Robert & Debbie Morris

Foreword by James & Betty Robison

The Blessed Marriage

Experiencing Heaven on Earth in Your Marriage

TABLE OF CONTENTS

This book is dedicated to Debbie's parents,
Grady and Edra Hughes.

To Grady W. Hughes:
For leaving us a rich heritage of love
by demonstrating love as a verb
expressed best in action.

To Edra Hughes:
For overcoming adversities with faith,
courageously facing the future
and always providing a warm and loving home.

The Blessed Marriage

Robert and Debbie Morris have been our friends and co-laborers for many years, and now they are our pastors. When they began writing this book, we knew a timely word from God was imminent. In a culture plagued by divorce, a loving and enjoyable marriage seems almost mythical. The statistics are so dismal that one must ask how a blessed marriage could possibly exist.

We cannot begin to count the number of times we have been asked, "Do you really get along like you do on television?" People do not seem to believe that two people who have lived together so long could still like each other, much less love each other. But after more than 40 years of marriage, we can honestly say that by God's abundant grace, we love and enjoy one another more today than ever before.

Husbands, if you are looking for three steps to make your wife happy so that you can go your own way, you will never find them. There is no miraculous way to enjoy a wife with whom you share no intimacy. There is no magic system for learning to love someone else more than you love yourself. Only God can take two hearts and teach them to beat as one. He wants your marriage to conform to His plan for blessing that will not only change your interaction with one another but will serve His Kingdom purposes as well.

Wives, if you expect your husband to be your ultimate source of joy and fulfillment, you will be disappointed every time. Betty knows firsthand the difficulty that comes with this kind of thinking. Only when she began believing that God truly loved her and started trusting in His love was she able to receive my love. Her faith in God's concern for her took the burden of making her happy off of my shoulders and freed us both to enjoy the adventure of following Christ together.

When we began our marriage, we had no plans to be on television together someday. With her shy and quiet demeanor, Betty was very content to remain completely out of the limelight while I preached. But God showed us that He wanted us to work together more visibly. He wanted Betty to co-host the LIFE TODAY television program. My sweet, shy wife allowed God to stretch her far outside of the comfortable niche in which she had always ministered; the result has been truly amazing.

Suddenly, our marriage and family were on display to the world. Never before had we ministered together so closely. And the more we work together, the more we are convinced that marriage is one of God's greatest gifts to mankind. When we are submitted to God's Word, our union is marked by His unfailing love. Any relationship built on such selfless love will grow into a life of abundant blessing.

Whether you are desperately seeking hope for a marriage on the verge of ruin or simply looking to restore life to a marriage stuck in the dull rut of routine, you will find answers in this book. Robert and Debbie's testimony will encourage and challenge you to walk away from defeat and toward victory in your marriage. As you read and submit to the truth in these pages, may you discover a truly blessed marriage.

— James and Betty Robison

CHAPTER 1

Marriage Is the Image of God

When we were first married, I (Robert) had no plan of making major changes to my social agenda in order to accommodate my bride. I have always loved sports and the outdoors: skiing, scuba diving, motorcycle riding, playing golf, hunting, you name it. I could not imagine life without these pleasures.

Well, it wasn't long before the competition for my time became an issue in our marriage. One night, we were up late, having a "discussion." You know about "discussions," don't you? They usually involve yelling, animated hand gestures and sometimes even tears. That's right . . . a "discussion." What it boiled down to was that Debbie had grown tired of playing second fiddle to my selfish obsession with entertainment. I, of course, saw nothing wrong with the way I had been acting. I thought it was selfish of her to want me to give up the things in my life that brought me pleasure.

At the climax of our discussion, Debbie looked at me with tears in her eyes and said, "Sometimes, with as little time as you spend with me, I wonder if you even love me." Young and immature, I responded quickly, but not very delicately, "You don't know if I love you? Look at the size of that ring on your finger!" Okay, now, twenty-some years later, I know that was an extremely shallow and insensitive remark. At that time though, I really believed I had proven my love enough by buying her an expensive ring. With a broken heart, Debbie looked at me, slipped the ring off her finger, set it on the night stand and said, "You can have it back if you will spend tomorrow with me."

We have come a long way since that discussion. Now, Debbie is the most important person in my life. When I'm stressed out, she encourages me to go play golf; and we go on hunting trips together. We are in love more today than the day we said, "I do." How did that squabbling couple go from disaster to blessing? God has transformed our hearts with His truth, and His Spirit has unified us and blessed us with amazing intimacy. He is so good, and we have discovered that His ways are perfect.

The Bliss of Eden

Has marriage always looked like it does in most American homes today? If hidden cameras followed typical Christian couples and typical non-Christian couples, would we be able to tell which marriages were unions of believers just by watching how they treated one another? Since mankind is fallen, is it even reasonable to hope for a union between man and woman that could bring anything but headaches and heartbreaks?

Let's look back to the Garden of Eden, where the first couple lived out the first marriage completely and exactly how God intended. What must it have looked like?

"In the beginning God created the heavens and the earth," (Genesis 1:1). On the sixth day, He created man. Although man enjoyed the utopia of the pre-cursed earth and the sweetest

3

communion with God possible, he was not content. However, his discontentment did not stem from a sinful attitude but from an earnest need. God had placed within him a craving for something else, someone else; man needed a companion. Even God, who was pleased with all that He had made, commented: "It is not good that man should be alone" (Genesis 2:18).

Now man was not completely alone. He lived in a zoo! In fact, his first job as ruler over God's creation was to name all of the animals. Secretly, he must have hoped that in getting to know the animals he would find one that would be a suitable companion. But alas, there were none on earth like him. Adam, the first man, can appreciate loneliness in a way none of us will ever know.

In tune with Adam's desires and needs, God stepped in as provider. He put Adam to sleep, took a rib from his side and created a woman from that rib. Upon waking, Adam gazed in wonder upon God's handiwork:

> *"This is now bone of my bones*
> *And flesh of my flesh;*
> *She shall be called Woman,*
> *Because she was taken out of Man."*
>
> *(Genesis 2:23)*

You know, Adam could have named her "Maid" or "Cook" or "Bambi," but he didn't. Their relationship was so pure that he was not looking for what she could do for him. Rather, he simply received her as the gift that she was. Woman had been created to fulfill the desire for companionship in his heart . . . and she did.

A more innocent era between man and woman has never existed. They were completely vulnerable with one another, naked and exposed. With nothing to hide, no sin to mar their intentions, no past to jade their expectations, Adam and Eve embarked on the beautiful adventure of marriage.

Can you imagine what a relationship would be like without the plagues of selfishness, ambition or rebellion? Adam and Eve must have thrived in absolute harmony and peace. Without sinful dispositions, they naturally put each other ahead of themselves. This was God's design for marriage. It was meant to be a place of service and tenderness. It was meant to bring joy and completion. In God's perfect creation, the union between man and woman was to be a safe place for them to fulfill their ultimate purposes by giving themselves completely to the other within the pleasure of absolute intimacy.

We're Not in Eden Anymore

Marriage took a nasty fall when Adam and Eve rebelled against God's perfect plan. When they separated themselves from God, they separated from one another as well. Selfishness, competition and immaturity not only took their toll on each one as individuals, these inadequacies made the perfect marriage unachievable. Now, millennia later, we find ourselves embracing divorce as a satisfactory resolution to sin problems within the home. We have come a long way since the Garden of Eden.

Divorce is not new though. It's been around almost as long as sin has . . . not by coincidence either. In Jesus' day, it was a hot topic of discussion. The Pharisees even tried to use it to trap Jesus in heresy. They came to Him and asked, "Is it lawful for a man to divorce his wife for *just* any reason?" (Matthew 19:3). Notice that the word "just" is in italics. That is because in the original Greek text, this word is not found. So, the question should read, "Is it lawful for a man to divorce his wife for *any* reason?" (emphasis added). The Pharisees knew the law, and they knew the interpretation of the law even better. They knew the allowances for divorce within the Jewish culture, and they hoped that Jesus would say something that would prove He was against God's law.

Jesus' response must have annoyed them though, because the first thing He said was, "Have you not read . . . ?" (Matthew 19:4). Now these were Pharisees, very learned religious men. They memorized the first five books of the Bible, knew them by heart. Of course they had read! Jesus knew, however, that though they had read, they had no understanding of the truth of marriage; otherwise, they would never have asked the question.

Jesus continued:

> *"Have you not read that He who made them at the beginning 'made them male and female,' and said, 'For this reason a man shall leave his father and mother and be joined to his wife, and the two shall become one flesh'? So then, they are no longer two but one flesh. Therefore what God has joined together, let not man separate."*
>
> *(Matthew 19:4-6)*

These are strong words. In today's society, they are fightin' words. Isaiah 59:19 tells us that,

> *When the enemy comes in like a flood,*
> *The Spirit of the Lord will lift up a*
> *standard against him.*

Even back in Bible times, Satan was attacking God's people using lies about the beauty and purpose of marriage. Jesus is God's Word in the flesh, and He will not tolerate deception.

Without apology or compromise, Jesus laid the truth before them. He looked these pious men right in the eyes and spoke the God-honest truth.

Despite Jesus' comeback, the Pharisees did not waver. They dug way back into their dogmatic law interpretations and asked another question: "Why then did Moses command to give a certificate of divorce, and to put her away?" (v. 7) Fair question. The Jews were supposed to live by the law, and Moses' law gave instructions for what a divorce should look like. Thinking they had Him cornered, the Pharisees asked how Jesus' words and Moses' words could possibly match up.

Jesus' answer to them is the same answer we need to hear today. "He said to them, 'Moses, because of the hardness of your hearts, permitted you to divorce your wives, but from the beginning it was not so'" (Matthew 19:8). Friends, divorce is always the result of hard-heartedness. In some divorces, there is one hard heart and one victim. In others, there are two hard hearts refusing to submit. Sometimes, the hard heart manifests itself through adultery. Other times, it drives the couple apart through desertion. Sadly, hardness of heart cripples faith that is essential for the survival of marriages. Wherever it shows up, a hard heart leads to divorce. God never intended for divorce to be an option out of marriage. Moses gave concession only because of the hardness of man's heart.

Go back to Jesus' words in Matthew 19:4-5. "Have you not read that He who made them at the beginning 'made them male and female' and said, 'For this reason a man shall leave his father and mother and be joined to his wife, and the two shall become one flesh'?" Jesus is referring back to the creation account, back to Genesis 1:27 and 2:24. In Genesis 1:27, we are told that God created male and female in His own image. It does not say that man was created in God's image but that male and female were. Men bear the image of God, and so do women.

Have you ever considered that God is both masculine and feminine? Both genders display attributes of God that are unique. As a single person, you can represent qualities of God the Father *or* God the Son *or* God the Holy Spirit. But as a single person, you cannot represent the Trinity. You are only one person, one gender.

Here is the truth about marriage that we have been building up to. This truth will change your perspective about marriage forever. It has the power to transform your relationship with your spouse. Living out the reality of this truth will make you a poignant witness of God's character to your children, your family, your neighbors and your church.

Are you ready for this? Marriage IS the very image of God. A married couple, submitted to the divine design for matrimony, will present a picture of God to the world. Because of sin, not every marriage can capture the beauty of the Godhead, but the union of two believers who are committed to letting the reality of the Trinity shine through their relationship will not only show the world what God is like, but these two who have become one will also enjoy the same intimacy that the Father, the Son and the Spirit share.

Did you catch that? God, the great Three-in-One, chose to reveal Himself to this world through your marriage relationship. If you allow Him to do so, He will bless your marriage with the benefits of heavenly companionship. This is God's ultimate desire for marriage. Two become one, just as He is one, bringing Him ultimate glory and channeling abundant blessing to their union and family. This is the blessed marriage.

Imaging God

Marriage is the image of God. Beautiful. It just sounds so poetic. It also sounds like a relationship far from what most couples experience every day. The Trinity is harmonious, complementary, functional and inviting. Do any of these words describe your marriage? They certainly didn't describe ours when we were first married!

Think back to your last disagreement, did it display harmony? What about your individual parenting styles? Would you say they complement one another? Do your day-to-day interactions result in a functioning lifestyle, or do you regularly feel dysfunctional because your differences make life seem impossible? Are people drawn to your home, drawn to relationship with your family? Does your marriage really look like God?

Mirroring God in our marriages cannot be a concept we simply admire. It must be a lifestyle we embrace. When lived out, mirroring God will communicate three extraordinary truths about the persona of God.

Having Your Head Screwed on Straight

First, marriage demonstrates equality that functions with order. Think about how the Trinity works. You have God the Father, God the Son and God the Holy Spirit. Which one is greater than the other? None. All three persons of the Trinity are totally equal. However, God the Father is the head of the Trinity. This is only possible if "head" refers to function and not to position. There is a difference.

The president of a bank is the head. He sits in the position of leadership, making more money, making all the decisions, asserting his will on all those underneath his control. In this sense, the head is a position from which he rules. However, God the Father does not position Himself over the Son and the Spirit. Instead, He functions as the head of their unity so that each can flourish in their individual roles. An example of this would be a partnership between a salesman and a supplier. In order for there to be a successful partnership, the supplier has to provide the salesman something to market. The supplier functions as the head of that partnership in that he is the source that the salesman draws from to do his job. In reality, neither can be successful without the other. They are equally important. In a similar fashion, God the Father is the source for the Son and the Spirit. They draw from Him all they need to achieve their full potentials.

Within marriage, God has established the husband to be the head of the wife. God does not position him over her with an iron fist and a call button. No, God places high expectation on that husband. He is to mirror the Father's role in the Trinity as the source in the relationship. The husband's function within the marriage is not boss. It's not lord, master or hot rod. It is source. Just as God is the husband's provider, the husband should provide for his wife financially, emotionally, mentally and spiritually.

Think of a husband as being head like a spring of water is the source of the water. A spring pushes water out of the ground. Get the picture? The function of the husband is to get under the wife and push her up. Her success depends on his obedience to be her source. Because of him she will either trickle up undetected, barely watering the inches of ground around the spring, or she will explode forth like Old Faithful, rocketing skyward, showering areas she never imagined before that she could reach. She is not less important than he. He is not greater than she. They are a team, equal in position but separate in function.

Sometimes the problem within marriage is not that it suffers from the "headless horseman" syndrome. Men are often blamed for not stepping up and taking the lead, but women just as often usurp the position of leader within the home creating an order not sanctioned by God. In these families, there is a constant battle with a "two-headed monster." God's design is for the husband to be the head. Wives who refuse to submit to this natural order generate constant frustration in their marital relationships as well as in their homes.

When unbelievers come into your home, when they live in close enough community with you to observe your marriage relationship, they should be amazed to see the equality that exists between you. The world doesn't think it is possible to have total equality in a marriage where the husband is the head. They think those two ideas are diametrically opposed. The problem is they have never been introduced to our God. He has thrived with headship and equality for all of eternity. Marriage gives us a chance to prove to a doubting world that the triune God exists and that His ways are perfect. Together, you and your spouse can exhibit the remarkable prosperity that is achieved when equality is lived out in submission to God's prescribed order.

Embracing Their Otherness

A second way that marriage reflects God is that it celebrates individuality within oneness. There are two different ways to define the word "one." The first describes a loneliness, as in being the only one: "There is only one piece of chocolate cake left. You better grab it while you can!"

The way a marriage is "one," however, really speaks of the unity achieved through its plurality. In other words, there cannot be oneness in marriage unless there are two individuals.

Our nephew played football in high school. In his senior year, he came up with a slogan for the team: "Eleven Hearts, One Goal." The school rallied behind that slogan, and it showed up on T-shirts and billboards and advertisements. People recognized the power behind eleven individuals joining together under the same goal. Even though there were eleven different men on the team with eleven different functions and eleven different strengths and eleven different weaknesses, they were all one team. On their jerseys, there was one name. On the field, they worked toward one goal. In the game, they performed from one playbook. In the end, they shared one trophy. They were a group of individuals coming together as one.

God is only one God, but He is also three very distinct persons. When we talk about Jesus, we think of the divine traits He displayed during His time on earth. He was humble, bold, kind and compassionate. God the Father may also have those characteristics, but when we think of Him, we relate to His fatherhood and headship. He is holy, loving, just and sovereign. The Holy Spirit is in a realm of His very own. We know Him as the comforting, empowering, mysterious one. They are all so unique, yet there is still only one God. They function in perfect unity not because they are all the same, but because their differences enable them to come together to complete the fullness of who they are as One.

Marriage, the surrendered marriage committed to mirroring God, will display the same quality. Men and women are very different. We are so different. When we watch a movie together, I (Robert) sit in awe of the talented five-year-old girl who cries so believably and of the camera angle that is so perfectly positioned that her tears glimmer under the lights. Debbie on the other hand bawls with the five-year-old because she is caught up in the story. We are different. When we shop, I (Debbie) love to look and try on and admire. It is a joy for me. Robert on the other hand tries to beat his best time for getting in and out of the store with as few casualties as possible. We are different. To fit both of our likings, a romantic evening would have to include a candlelit dinner out followed by watching the game on the big screen TV with a bowl of popcorn spilled on the floor because we jumped up and cheered the game-winning point. We are different.

Our differences and individuality do not have to be surrendered to experience unity. In fact, they should not be sacrificed. By celebrating one another's differences and using those strengths and passions to build up your marriage, you mirror the same type of unity in which the Trinity has thrived for all of time. Satan wants to convince you that your spouse's peculiarities will only weaken your marriage and thus you should do all you can to change that person to be more like you. Wrong! Choosing unity, striving for unity through the challenges of your differences, exhibits obedience to the calling God placed on marriage when He first created it. You will find yourself on a road to a more blessed marriage because together you are fulfilling the purpose of representing a triune God, individuals bound together as One because of their uniqueness.

Never Saying Quit

Finally, marriage represents the image of God when one rests under the guarantee of total commitment. God the Father, God the Son and God the Holy Spirit will never split up. They will never get a divorce. They are totally committed to one another.

In the Matthew 19 passage we looked at earlier, Jesus comes across somewhat perturbed that the Pharisees would even ask Him a question about tolerating divorce. You see, Jesus knew the original purpose of marriage; He knew God's intent for man and woman to represent Him to the world through marriage. Because He knew this, the very idea that men would consider representing God to the world through divorce exasperated Him. This would communicate that God is a covenant breaker, and God is not a covenant breaker.

> *"For the LORD God of Israel says*
> *That He hates divorce,*
> *For it covers one's garment with violence,"*
> *Says the LORD of hosts.*
> *"Therefore take heed to your spirit,*
> *That you do not deal treacherously."*
> *(Malachi 2:16)*

God hates divorce. Now, read that again: God hates divorce. He does not hate divorced people. He hates divorce because it covers people with violence. God loves people, and God loves marriage. He created marriage. But divorce was never God's plan for marriage. He never intended husbands and wives, children and grandchildren to have to suffer through its agony.

If the Bible said that God hated car wrecks, it wouldn't mean that He hated people who had been involved in car accidents. He would hate car wrecks because car wrecks hurt people. In the same way, He hates divorce because He loves people and divorce hurts people. God loves people, and thus He hates divorce. His plan for marriage far exceeded what most people settle for today.

Divorce not only hurts people, it offends God. When a couple goes into marriage reserving the right to divorce if things go wrong, they misrepresent God because He is totally committed to the unity of the Trinity.

Please understand that when you decide that divorce will be an option for your marriage if your spouse ever . . . (fill in the blank yourself), you tell Satan exactly how to attack your spouse in order to destroy your marriage. We challenge you to renew your marriage vows today with new fervor. Choose to mimic the example of the Trinity by promising one another that divorce will never be an option. Decide today that no matter what your husband does, no matter what your wife does, you will not choose divorce. Disarm Satan. Take away the ammunition he aims at your spouse. Instead, invite God's help and blessing into your marriage to see it sustained and victorious.

God has entrusted us with the privilege and responsibility

to exemplify His character to a world that doesn't understand Him. As individuals we carry attributes of the Father, Jesus or the Holy Spirit. But as married couples, we can give the world a glimpse of the Trinity: three unique persons, functioning equally under the headship of the Father, forever committed to unity with one another. The Father, Son and Holy Spirit are reaching out to a dying world. Your marriage has a part in the world coming to know! Approaching your marriage relationship with this purpose in mind should give you renewed focus and energy to live pleasing before God.

Over the next nine chapters, we want to share some truths God has taught us over twenty-six years of marriage that have brought blessing into our lives. God wants to bless your marriage too because He knows a blessed marriage will represent a more accurate picture of Himself. Open your hands, open your hearts and receive the encouragement we desire to pass on to you.

Jesus' first miracle was at a wedding, changing water to wine. Water represents survival. Wine represents joy. Allow Jesus to work in your marriage a miracle of transformation that will take it from mere survival to incredible joy.

CHAPTER 2

Becoming One

God has placed a high calling on marriages to reflect Him, but how in the world do we get to a place where we can do that? We have learned that there is only one way to honor our Maker and become one: Both of us have to die.

Now please, don't close the book and give up on us just yet. We realize that death was not the marriage alternative you were looking for when you picked up this book. But think about it for a minute. If you have a relationship with God today, you received it through death. Jesus died for you. His death gave you life. And you only received the life He offered by choosing to die as well.

Worldly logic tells us that death only brings grief, finality and loss. Death should be mourned, not embraced. Only when we have Kingdom vision does the truth about death come alive. Just as Jesus' death opened the door of life to millions who would follow Him, your choice to die will open the door to new life in your marriage.

Unlocking the Door to Blessing

In the last chapter, we looked at Jesus' conversation with some Pharisees about divorce. In that conversation, He referenced God's original instructions to married couples given just after Eve was created from Adam's rib:

Therefore a man shall leave his father

and mother and be joined to his wife,
and they shall become one flesh.

(Genesis 2:24)

The phrase "they shall become one flesh" is found five times in Scripture. After God coins it in Genesis, Jesus quotes it in Matthew 19 and in Mark 10 to help clarify the Father's intent for marriage. In Ephesians 5, Paul refers back to it in his instructions to husbands and wives. So, in these four quotations, the phrase "they shall become one flesh" applies to the marital relationship.

The fifth usage of this phrase puts a twist on it that we weren't expecting. In 1 Corinthians 6:16, Paul says:

Or do you not know that he who is joined
to a harlot is one body with her? For "the
two," He says, "shall become one flesh."

In the other four passages, the two "becoming one flesh" highlighted the unity of a married couple. Here though, "they shall become one flesh" shifts the focus from the unity to the flesh. Paul points out that when a man has sex with a harlot, he becomes one flesh with her.

Does this bother you? Until now, we have seen the two becoming one flesh as a significant symbol of godly unity, but here it has been cheapened. Sex makes a husband and wife one flesh, but it makes a husband and harlot one flesh as well.

Let's read on. The very next verse says:

But he who is joined to the Lord is
one spirit with Him. (v. 17)

As a child of God, you have a close relationship with the Lord. Your relationship with Him is not a physical one, but a spiritual one. You joined your spirit with His to become one with Him. Dear couple, this is the higher calling of marriage as well. If you have been married longer than a week, you know that coming together physically does not give you a successful marriage. Sex is not the key to oneness! Becoming one spirit, however, is.

So, how did you become one spirit with the Lord? We've already said it, you died. You died to your will, your desires and your way. So, how can you become one spirit with your spouse? You die. For you to have a successful marriage, both of you must die. You must be able to say, "I'll die so that you can live." This means that you die to your agenda. You yield the right of way. You step down from first place and lift your spouse up instead.

What would it look like if you joined your spirit with your spouse's spirit and the two of you joined with the Spirit of God and all three of you were moving in the same direction, unified with the same purpose? Do you think that would look like a successful marriage? You bet it would!

Because of our role in ministry, we have had the opportunity to counsel many couples. We've discovered something after hours and hours of listening and advising: The problem with marriage counseling today is that we are counseling living people. Marriage counseling would not even be necessary if both the husband and wife would just die. We have never met a couple with a marriage problem that could not be resolved with this therapy. When a husband decides to die for his wife and a wife decides to die for her husband, all the problems are solved.

Did you know that God designed marriage to help you die? He did not give you your spouse so that you could be happy and in love and grow old with him or her. His greatest desire for you is that you die to self. Why? Because the Bible tells us that God's plan for our lives is to become like Jesus. When you die to self and live for your spouse, you look like Jesus. And, by the way, you are also happy and in love!

As believers, what happens when our bodies die? We go to heaven. Well, guess what. The same thing happens in our marriages when we die – we go to heaven. Marriage becomes heaven on earth when we die to ourselves. Heaven is heaven because it is a community of people who act like Jesus. Your home could be the same type of place: two people living like Jesus, enjoying the bliss of heaven on earth.

Marriage Is not a Contract

American society is a contract society. When you get a job, you sign an employment contract. When you buy a house, you sign a mortgage. When you buy a car, you sign a loan agreement. The goal of every contract is to protect your rights and limit your responsibilities. A contract sets the boundaries that you are obligated to act within, but it also sets expectations upon the other party and provides an outlet for you if the contract specifications are not met.

As Americans, we are so used to entering contracts that we have carried the contract spirit into our marriages. While there is no legal document the husband and wife sign on their wedding day that sets specific parameters or expectations, you can be sure the contract stands firm in their hearts and minds. Most attitudes in the home go something like this: "Don't ask too much of me. I still have the right to be my own person, and I will not give up my life. If this marriage requires more than I am willing to give, I am out of here."

Marriages cannot survive with a contract spirit. They will undoubtedly end in divorce. If Jesus is our example of how we are to treat our spouses, we must come to them with the same attitude with which Jesus came. Philippians 2:5-8 paints a beautiful picture of Jesus' example:

Let this mind be in you which was also in

Christ Jesus, who, being in the form of God, did not consider it robbery to be equal with God, but made Himself of no reputation, taking the form of a bondservant, and coming in the likeness of men. And being found in appearance as a man, He humbled Himself and became obedient to the point of death, even the death of the cross.

Jesus came in humility, with a desire to serve. His motivation did not lie in what He deserved but in what it would take to make relationship with His bride possible. What it took was His very life. Jesus came to make a covenant with us not to enter a contract.

To rid yourself of the contract spirit, you must be willing to lay down your rights. When you were single, you looked out for yourself, you took care of yourself and you kept everything precious and valuable to yourself. As individuals, we protect our rights to priority, ownership and privacy. In order to become one, you have to lay those rights down.

Looking Out for Number One

The first step to freeing your spouse from your contract spirit is to lay down your right to priority. You can no longer be the most important person in your life. You can no longer seek to meet your needs first. You must demote anything in your life that is more important to you than your spouse. In essence, this is the promise you must make: "I give you the right to be the first priority in my life and to give up anything you perceive as competition."

In Genesis 2:24, when God saw Adam and Eve together and said, "Therefore a man shall leave his father and mother and be joined to his wife," He was not talking to Adam and Eve. They did not even know what a mother and father were! God wanted us to know that when we marry, we must leave the most significant relationship in our lives and elevate our spouse to that place.

What has priority in your life right now? What does your spouse think has priority in your life? What are you willing to give up in order to achieve the oneness you need to experience heaven on earth? Laying down your right to priority is the essential first step to bringing blessing into your home.

What's Mine Is Ours

The second right you have to lay down in your marriage is the right to ownership. There is no "mine"; there is only "ours." Selfish people cannot have a successful marriage. It will never work. The "mine" and "yours" attitude builds a wall between you, and two cannot become one if there is a wall between them.

Ownership applies to more areas of your life than you might

think. Of course, it applies to money and possessions. Women who think, "What he makes is ours, but what I make is mine," have not laid down their right to ownership. Men who isolate their stuff in a corner of the garage with a loud "Do Not Touch" sign attached have not laid down their right to ownership.

But laying down the right to ownership extends beyond the material. One thing we all own is our bodies, and we usually cling to our rights over our bodies unto death. 1 Corinthians 7:4 says:

> *The wife does not have authority over her own body, but the husband does. And likewise the husband does not have authority over his own body, but the wife does.*

Men, I am sure you are saying, "She can have authority over this body any time she wants!" Well okay then, get up off the couch and take the garbage out like she's asked you to a hundred times. If she owns your body, go mow the lawn, loosen the jar lid and reach to the top shelf. Your body is not only hers in bed, it's hers when she needs an extra hand, a little help or stronger muscles. You belong to her.

Women, are you shouting "Amen!"? Well, before you get too excited, remember that the verse goes two ways. Your body is not your own either. He may not need you to take out the trash or run to the store, but he does need your body.

Men have a need for sex. They don't just have a desire or craving, they have a need. In fact, surveys show that sex is one of man's greatest needs, second only to honor. When your husband needs your body, it is not yours to deny. You must lay down the right to your body and place priority on his need. Lay down the right to ownership. What's mine is ours.

An Open Book

The last right you have to be willing to lay down is your right to privacy. After you say "I do," there is nothing in your past, nothing in your closet, nothing in your future from which your spouse should be restricted. You must give the right to free and unhindered access to every aspect of your life, including the right to complain about or confront you on any issue without the fear of retaliation.

Before sin entered the world, Adam and Eve "were both naked, the man and his wife, and were not ashamed" (Genesis 2:25). Secrecy only brings shame. Marriage should be a place of acceptance and encouragement. It should be a haven where each can come just as they are, with their history and their hopes, to find a loving embrace with no questions asked. With such a sanctuary to retreat to, marriage can achieve the intimacy God intended.

You can only have a place of refuge if both parties agree to lay down their insensitivities and their insecurities. If your spouse is truly your first priority, you will seek to communicate with him or her in a gentle, patient and accommodating manner. When your husband (or wife) speaks to you or responds to you in a way that comes across harsh, choose to trust his (or her) heart of love toward you and ask for clarification. Don't allow Satan to rob you of the sweet gift of intimacy. Lay down your right to privacy and embrace one another with the highest favor.

Marriage Is a Covenant

Jesus came, laying down His right to be praised by all of creation, submitting to the Father's plan for His crucifixion and revealing His heart of love to the world. But even more than that, Jesus took up our responsibilities. We were all accountable for our sins and faced judgment which assured separation from God. Jesus came to pick up those responsibilities and carry them for us. He paid for our sins and took judgment for us. You see, Jesus did not come to fulfill a contract; He came to enter a covenant.

"Covenant" means "to cut." Jesus was cut for us, and His sacrifice told us that He had not only given up all His rights for us, He also had taken up all of our responsibilities. Are you willing to be cut for your spouse? God designed marriage to be a covenant. When He created Eve, He literally cut Adam's side, took a rib and made her from him. A covenant was cut. Entering your marriage with a spirit of covenant says, "I will give up all my rights in order to meet your needs, even to the point of death. I will also assume great responsibility for the success of our marriage."

In a contract, you are free from obligation if the other party does not live up to the agreement. In a covenant, however, you commit to take up all the responsibility, so no matter what your spouse does, there is no out. All the responsibility is yours. A covenant is irrevocable, unconditional and unbreakable. Jesus can't take back His blood on the cross. God never goes back on His promises. It is not in His character to break a covenant. As our marriages mirror God, we too must be committed to the covenants we make with our spouses. That not only means laying down all of our rights, but it also means picking up some specific responsibilities that nurture the relationship and make it durable.

The Greatest of These Is Love

Above all, when you step into a covenant with your spouse, you are committing to pick up the responsibility to love. Because God is love and because you have received His love through Jesus, you should love with the love of Christ. Practically speaking, you must learn to love according to Christ's standard, no matter what. And when you fall short of that standard (and you undoubtedly will), you commit never to justify your behavior.

Why is this so hard? It's the "no matter what" that makes it challenging. We choose to love one another no matter what

mood we are in, no matter what the circumstances, no matter
what the response, no matter how we feel. No matter what! We
are not used to this kind of love, well, at least not giving this
kind of love. Jesus loves each of us exactly like this every day,
and we receive it freely. But when it comes to giving it freely,
we complain that it is too heavy a burden.

Usually, we choose to love when the other person is acting
the way we like or when we feel particularly warm and fuzzy
or when we want the other person to do something for us. This
is not the love Jesus modeled. This is the worldly model of love
that consequently is not even real love. Worldly love is actually
self love. Loving yourself is not picking up the responsibility of
another. It is clinging to your own rights.

For example, husbands, have you ever had this conversation
in your head? "She wants me to do what for her? How can she
expect me to go out of my way when she is so disrespectful to
me? I mean, she doesn't even appreciate that I work hard every
day to give her this life. The day I do that for her is the day she
gives me a little recognition."

What about you, wives? Does this sound familiar? "If he
touches me one more time . . . Doesn't he see the anger on my
face? I mean, he walks in here, ignoring the kids, sits down in
front of the TV without so much as a 'how was your day?' and
then wants me to fall all over him when the lights go out. Well,
he can just forget it!"

Husbands, wives, God does not hold you responsible for how your spouse treats you, but He will require you to answer for how you treat him or her. Covenant commits to love no matter what, in action or reaction, in word, deed or thought.

Reach for the Stars

God has a wonderful plan for your spouse. He has gifted each of you with amazing talents and granted you both dreams to make an impact on this world. When you enter into the marriage covenant, you pick up the responsibility to do everything possible to help the other reach his or her highest potential and achieve God's perfect will. You become God's partner in seeing your beloved's dreams fulfilled.

God designed man to reach his potential with a woman helping him. And He designed woman to reach her potential with a man helping her. Unbelievers will not understand this, but it is true. Feminists in particular will find this offensive. Since the fall of mankind, men have mistreated women. Not willing to stand for mistreatment any longer, women stopped trusting men to take care of them. They began teaching their daughters that men will fail them so they better learn to make it through life without any help. It is understandable that women have come to such conclusions, but that does not make their conclusions right. If men would begin to love women as Christ loves the church, if they would begin to honor them and motivate them to reach their full potential, women would disarm, and the feminist movement would dissolve.

When you stand before God and give an account of your life, He will ask you what you did with the most precious gift He ever gave you. You will be responsible for the success of your husband or wife. What will you have to say? Your destiny is not all wrapped up in what you do and what you become. What becomes of your spouse impacts your destiny too. Be a blessing. As your husband reaches for the stars, cheer him on. As your wife climbs that ladder of success, give her a boost.

Live by the Word

Many women in the church despise Ephesians 5 because it commands them to submit to their husbands. Even the strongest Christian women have struggled with that command. Men can help their wives understand and live up to this standard by looking back a few verses and joining in her humility. Before he tells women to submit, Paul challenges all believers, " . . . be filled with the spirit . . . submitting to one another in the fear of God" (Ephesians 5:18, 21). The third responsibility we must be willing to pick up in marriage is to submit to one another. You must say to your spouse, "I assume the responsibility to serve you by first submitting my life to the Lordship of Jesus Christ and by surrendering to His Word as the standard for my life and our marriage and family." Marriage is to be mutually submissive, as you first submit to God and then commit to serve one another.

Every relationship will struggle through conflict. The test for a covenant marriage is what you do with that conflict. It has been estimated that less than one-third of Christian couples use the Bible to resolve conflict. That means that not one out of every three Christian marriages relies on the Word of God to settle their differences. As Christians, we say we believe that the Bible is the source of truth and contains applicable direction for our lives, but when we disagree, do we turn to it?

Jesus told us that the greatest commandment is to love God and the second greatest commandment is to love others as we love ourselves. The Bible tells husbands to love their wives as Christ loves the church and tells wives to respect their husbands as the head of the home. These are very clear directives in Scripture that could clear up a lot of arguments right away. The Bible is full of wisdom waiting to be tested and proven valid in our lives. We just have to go to the Word when we find ourselves on different sides of the fence on an issue.

A person committed to a contract marriage would enter a fight to prove he or she is right. In a covenant marriage, however, the right to priority already has been laid down, while the responsibilities to love and honor and submit have been picked up. Conflict should drive you to discover what God says is best for your marriage. If you are concerned that approaching conflict in such a passive manner will make you a doormat, remember who your defender is. Jesus is committed to you. He wants to work all things together for your good. But if you step in and attempt to make everything better in your life or your spouse's life, you rob Jesus of the opportunity. Only He can change your spouse. Only He can change you. When you commit to submission in your marriage, you give Him the control. When He is at the wheel in your marriage, you can trust that He will drive you places only wisdom and blessing can access.

We realize that both you and your spouse may not be crazy about this idea of dying to self and living in covenant. It is very possible that you will need to step out by faith in obedience to become the kind of husband or wife you are supposed to be in order to save your marriage. Every covenant has to have a redeemer. *The redeemer is the person who dies first.* Jesus was our Redeemer. Romans 5:8 says:

> *But God demonstrates His own love toward us, in*
> *that while we were still sinners, Christ died for us.*

Jesus died for us before we died to our sin. He died first and redeemed us from our selfishness!

Your relationship needs a redeemer. Are you be willing to die first? Will you lay down your rights and pick up the other person's responsibilities? If you are in a bad marriage, commit to being the redeemer. Commit to do your part even if the other person doesn't. Usher the spirit of covenant into your marriage, and kick the spirit of contract out. Do the right thing no matter what, and God will bless you!

I (Robert) remember another *discussion* Debbie and I had a few years ago. It had escalated to a point far beyond where it should have been. We were just going at it, and somehow in the midst of it I heard God speak. He said, "Shut up." Please don't be offended that God talks like that; He's only so abrupt because I am so hard-headed. Anyway, He told me to shut up, and of course I responded with, "But, but, but." Again He said, "Shut up." I argued, "But God, I'm right!" I'll never forget His response. "Do you want to be *right*, or do you want to be *right with Debbie?*"

Give up the rights of priority, ownership and privacy. Pick up the responsibilities of love, honor and submission. Begin living out the covenant of marriage by dying to yourself. Nothing justifies an unloving husband, and nothing justifies a dishonoring wife. If you have a bad marriage, put medicine on it, not salt. A loving husband can heal a dishonoring wife. An honoring wife can heal an unloving husband. Trust God to bring your marriage to a place of death so that your home can become the dwelling place of Christ.

What lies beyond death for a believer is paradise. What lies beyond death for a believer's marriage is heaven on earth.

CHAPTER 3

This book is intimidating. All this talk of looking like God and dying to self is overwhelming. I mean, who can really meet such high expectations? Well, if there is one thing I know about men, it is that we love a challenge. I believe that while the thought of changing and dying might scare you to death, you can rise to the occasion. God did not set you up for failure! In fact, He wants so intensely for you to succeed in your marriage that He has given you every resource you need to make it: instruction from His Word, ability through His Spirit and confidence in His promises.

Joshua was no stranger to huge responsibility. He was charged with leading Israel into the Promised Land. Talk about an intimidating task. Israel was a nomadic tribe of nobodies walking into territory occupied by giants, protected by mighty warriors and inhabited by strong, established nations. God had told Israel that this land would be theirs, but it would only come with a fight.

Before Moses died, he passed the mantle of leadership on to Joshua. Three times he charged Joshua to be strong (Deuteronomy 31:6-8). After Moses died, God Himself came to Joshua with the same message, telling him three more times: "Be strong and very courageous . . . " (Joshua 1:6-9). When Joshua stood before the people for the first time as their leader, they affirmed the call on his life, "Just as we heeded Moses in all things, so we will heed you," and again he heard: "Only be strong and of good courage" (Joshua 1:17-18). If I were Joshua, I think I would have turned on my heel and high-tailed it out of there! Seven exhortations to be strong, what was he in for? Obviously, if Joshua wanted to lead Israel to victory, he would have to be strong.

Men are supposed to be strong, not strong in a macho, dominating, muscle-shirt way, but strong like Jesus. We should be strong in character, in conviction, in maturity and in humility. Society might tell us that a strong leader will claw, climb and manipulate his way to the top. But Jesus' example demonstrates that it takes a stronger man to swim against the currents of popular culture and choose to follow God instead.

Just before King David died, he had some very strong words of encouragement for his son Solomon:

> *Be strong, therefore, and prove yourself a man. And keep the charge of the Lord your God: to walk in His ways, to keep His statutes, His commandments, His judgments, and His testimonies.*
>
> *(1 Kings 2:2-3)*

Do you want to prove your manhood? Be strong in God. Obey and submit to His ways.

Peter describes the woman as the "weaker vessel" (1 Peter 3:7) implying that we as men need to be strong. Let me give you another word for strong: meek. Women are the weaker vessels, and men should be the meeker vessels. Meekness is strength under control. The root word for "meek" in the Greek implies the action of putting a bit in a horse's mouth. A horse is a strong animal, and placing a bit in his mouth does not sap his strength. The bit tames that power so that it can be directed. In the same manner, God wants to channel your strength not take it from you. In fact, in those areas where you are weak, He wants to pour His power into you. For your strength to reach its utmost potential, it must be tamed, under control. As a meek leader, you possess the required strength to lead your family and the necessary control to direct them to godliness.

Strong in Spirit

> *It is God who arms me with strength,*
> *And makes my way perfect.*
> *He makes my feet like the feet of a deer,*
> *And sets me on my high places.*
> *He teaches my hands to make war,*
> *So that my arms can bend a bow of bronze.*
>
> *(Psalm 18:32-34)*

David was mighty in battle, a man's man. Women danced and sang of him, "Saul has slain his thousands, And David his ten thousands" (1 Samuel 18:7). His reputation preceded him throughout all of Israel and beyond. Though his deeds were heroic and the people praised him profusely, he refused to hog the glory for himself. He knew the reason for his success. At heart, he knew he was just a shepherd boy whom God had granted favor. David knew that without God, he would be nothing.

Remember back in the first chapter when we referred to the Trinity as having equality with headship? Just as God the Father is head of the Trinity and yet still equal to the Son and the Spirit, so you should be with your wife. Do you remember what the meaning of "head" is? It is source. You are the spring that gets beneath your wife and pushes her up. That is a demanding responsibility, requiring strength and endurance. Fortunately, we are not left without a source. In 1 Corinthians 11:3 the Word says, "the head of every man is Christ, the head of woman is man." Jesus is our source. He wants to get beneath us and push us up. In Him, we have everything we need to be the source for our wives.

Now, here's the catch. For Jesus to be your source and strength, you have to know Him. You can't just know about Him, you have to go deep with Him. Somewhere along the way, men in the church became convinced that it is sissy to be intimate with their Savior. This is why some men freeze like blocks of ice during the worship portion of a church service.

Explain this to me: Why do men stand around like zombies on Sunday morning during church and act wild on Sunday afternoon during the football game? Let's think about this. Eleven men commit their lives to a game where it is their sole objective to get a ball across a line. These eleven men practice every day for hours, toiling and sweating. Then, once a week, they get on a plane to go hundreds of miles to find eleven other men who are going to try to stop them from getting that precious ball over the line. Then, fifty to seventy thousand men gather to watch these 22 players battle it out. And what do these men do when their team gets the ball over the line? They jump up, hands in the air, shouting, clapping and dancing. You know this is true because you've done it. I know it because I've done it!

Although there is nothing wrong with sports enthusiasm, it should cause us to look at our worship. In the Bible, worship is not a passive activity. We are commanded to clap and shout (Psalm 47:1) and to lift up our hands to bless the Lord (Psalm 134:2). If we can do it for the Steelers, why can't we do it for the One who died for us?

Men should be the greatest worshippers in the church, not women. The church has been over-mothered and under-fathered for years. A mother nurtures and cares; a father calls you to your destiny. Today we have a lot of weak men in the church because they have received all the nurturing without the instruction. These men don't worship because no man ever showed them the strength of praising God.

God says that He inhabits the praises of His people (Psalm 22:3). If you want God to be present and active in your home, praise Him. He is just waiting for the invitation. And when the music starts in church, I hope you turn to the person next to you and say, "Excuse me, but I am about to have a fit. You might want to move over a bit because you could get hurt." Let's be passionate in the praise of our Lord.

I already mentioned what a great warrior King David was. He killed a lion and a bear with his bare hands. One stone from David's slingshot toppled Goliath! To win his wife, he killed two hundred men in battle. David was a man's man, but he was also an extravagant worshipper. He wasn't ashamed to dance in front of others as he worshipped. Because he was secure in his manhood, David never held back when he worshipped. He praised God with all of his heart and strength.

Brothers, a good marriage is hard work, and so much of the responsibility falls on your shoulders. My prayer for you is that you will follow David's example and look to God to arm you with the strength you need to live up to the challenge and the endurance you need to go all ten rounds. Spend time in worship, connecting to the Father's heart so that His strength will empower your relationships with your wife and kids.

Strong on Your Knees

Women love to tease men about their refusal to stop and ask for directions. They just don't understand. I mean, I may be three hours late, but I will find it on my own. This is a matter of honor! A man knows how to read a map. A man has an innate sense of direction. A man should never need to ask another man what he already knows how to do. You never admit defeat to a fellow soldier.

Now this attitude might be tolerable when you are looking for a new restaurant, but when it comes to asking God for directions, get ready to be humbled. Pride is the opposite of prayer. Pride says, "I can do this on my own." Prayer says, "There is no way I can do this on my own." The truth of the matter is, you can't do marriage on your own. Your wife is too mysterious, and Satan is too mischievous. Stop seeing prayer as weakness; see it as empowerment. God honors our faith when we come to Him with our needs, and you will know that you can do more for your family through prayer than through any attempt you make in your own strength.

You should be the chief intercessor for your home. Even if your wife has the gift of prayer, you still have more authority in prayer than she does when it comes to your family. As the head, the source, God looks to channel blessing through you. Seek those blessings consistently and fervently in prayer.

Every year, God gives me a special gift. About twenty years ago, Debbie and I began giving God an extravagant gift at Christmas. We were convicted that if we gave holiday gifts to everyone else, why not share a gift for Jesus on his birthday? So, we started giving an extravagant gift every December. Well, when I started doing this, God came to me and said, "I'd like to give you a gift as well. Every year, ask me for something big. Make that your prayer request every day throughout the year, and let me bless you." I was blown away, but I did not turn down His offer.

One particular year, God asked me what I wanted, and I told Him that I really wanted to see my children fall in love with Jesus. I prayed for that every day. God is so good. That year, my kids fell in love with Jesus! My oldest son started coming to me and saying things like, "Dad, did you know that the Bible is really good?" I'd say, "Oh, really? Wow, I didn't know that, son. I've never read it." No, really I'd say, "Yes, yes, it is, son." And he'd share how he was learning to live the Bible every day because it is so practical. I began watching him in worship and I noticed that he was falling in love with Jesus. My middle son was fifteen that year, and he accepted Christ as his Savior. He had made a profession of faith at age five, but it was obvious to me that he really needed to be radically saved, and that year, he was. My daughter was young, but I saw it in her life too. She fell in love with Jesus. God worked mightily in the lives of my children in response to my prayers for them. That was the most precious gift I received that year, and I believe it was a precious gift to my children as well.

What about your kids? Are they acting out in rebellion? Are they in bondage to sin that is devastating their lives? Do their attitudes toward you reek with disrespect? Are they hurting through their adolescent years, insecure and lonely? Pray for them. They won't always come to you for help, but that doesn't mean you can't be their greatest ally on earth. Lift them up and watch the Father do amazing things in their lives.

Do the same for your wife as well. Are there attitudes and habits in your wife's life that you know dishonor God? Does she have potential that is untapped because of timidity or missed opportunities? Perhaps she just has a demanding schedule that exhausts her daily and needs extra energy and motivation. Whatever her need, you are her source; begin by interceding on her behalf before the One who can heal her, provide for her, help her and encourage her.

One word of warning: Be aware that God's answers to your prayers for your family might not be what you expect. Know that as you pray for them, God might just change *you* and show *you* how to be the answer your family is looking for. Remember, you are His representative in your home, so you will often be the very funnel He channels His blessings through. For example, maybe your son's low self-esteem will be healed by extra time and words of encouragement from you. Maybe your wife's hectic schedule can be relieved by you providing her with a once-a-week maid to come clean the house. Sometimes He will step in without any action from you and deal with the issue; but as you pray, be open to allowing God to use you in the lives of your family. If you are the problem, let Him fix you. If you are not the problem, let Him use you.

Strong in Leadership

John Maxwell teaches us that "leadership is influence."[1] Called to be a leader in your home, you are called to influence your family. As you are strong in praise, you not only will influence the spiritual atmosphere in your home; you teach your family how to worship God. As you are strong in prayer, you not only pull the blessings of God into their lives, but you also set an example of how to live dependently upon the Father.

When my son, Josh, was about five or six years old, I would meet him at his bedside every night for prayers. One night, I became a bit bored with his prayers because he said the same things every night. I complained to God a little about the situation, and He responded rather quickly, "Well, who has been teaching him to pray? You say the same things every night too! 'Lord, bless Josh. Protect him. Help him in school.'" You see, I was too busy to really teach my son to pray. I wanted to say a prayer and get him to sleep so that I could go find Mama. "Son, let's say these prayers, you get under your covers and don't come into my bedroom!" You know where I'm coming from. But that night, God showed me what my selfishness was teaching, or rather not teaching, my son about prayer. So, I never corrected Josh or told him how he should be praying. Instead, I began praying with him the same way I prayed in private. When I stopped praying in vain repetition, he stopped praying in vain repetition. As I became more fervent in prayer, so did he. Before long, Josh began praying powerful, passionate prayers: "Lord, I just ask you to help Dad in Jesus' name. Bless him, Lord. Help him at work. Help him to preach well . . . "

You see, as husband and father, you are the pastor in your home. The preacher at your church is not your wife's pastor. The children and youth ministers at your church are not your kids' pastors. You are the pastor for your family. The church staff only sees your family once or twice a week. What are you doing with them the rest of the time?

As the senior pastor at Gateway Church, I take seriously my responsibility to come alongside the men of the church and equip them with truth, faith and practical counsel for daily living.

The men in my church have to take what they receive and pass it on. The Bible says in 2 Timothy 2:2:

> *And the things that you have heard from me among many witnesses, commit these to faithful men who will be able to teach others also.*

My job is to pass on what I have received to you. As a faithful man, your job is to teach your family.

A good teacher doesn't just use words as his tool; he uses his life. To really influence your family, you have to get involved in their lives. God holds you accountable for what becomes of your wife and children. So when there are decisions to be made and problems to be solved, you should be right in the middle of them. I realize that your wife is quite capable of doing things herself, but she wants to be led. When you ask how her day went, and she explodes on you with stories of temperamental kids, rude repair men and mountains of laundry, she is crying out for you to get involved. Come to her rescue! Beat the kids, and then take her out to dinner. (I'm just kidding about beating the kids.)

When Debbie and I moved here to start a church, we had to decide what to do about our children's school. Our daughter was still elementary age, so we decided to home school her . . . we could handle third grade math. Our son, James, on the other hand, was in tenth grade, and we knew that was over our heads. So, we decided to check into local private schools. When it came down to doing the actual research, I was too busy, so I asked Debbie to do it. She didn't like going about it alone, but I insisted. She checked into several schools and picked one that required payment up front. So, we shelled out $5000.

James wasn't in school a few weeks before we realized that we had made a huge mistake. The school was very difficult with seven hard subjects requiring a great deal of him both in and out of the classroom. Now James is an outdoorsman: hunting, fishing, sports. He is very smart, but he doesn't do well when being rushed. He was so unhappy and wasn't flourishing in that environment at all. So, we pulled him out and put him in another school where he excelled. The $5000, however, was not so easily recovered. It was non-refundable. Needless to say, I was upset. I felt like Debbie had made a really bad call that cost us a lot of money.

The next morning, I was praying. As I was talking to God about something, I don't remember what, He interrupted me. In His familiar blunt voice, He said, "You lost $5000." Without delay, I disagreed and replied, "No, Debbie lost $5000." His response stung: "Oh, is she the head of this house now? Who is the head of this house?" I didn't have an answer for His questions. He continued, "Don't you ever get too busy to check out the school for your children! I knew this was going to happen." That may sound harsh, but I got the message: I am to be involved in my family. Every decision made that affects them will be traced back to me.

What about you? Are you the leader in your home? I've known lots of men who are strong and committed at work, but leave the family to their wives. That is a grave mistake. You will reap some serious consequences if you shirk family responsibility. You are to be strong. Stand in the gap for your family, sharing in their lives, fighting for their best, leading them to holiness. Strong leadership today boasts abundant blessing tomorrow.

Leaving a Legacy

Moses lived an exceptional life, used by God in ways most of us envy. There is a story in Exodus about him though that has a lot to say to us husbands and fathers.

After the burning bush experience, Moses prepared to return to Egypt. God had faithfully told him where to go, what to do, what to say and what miracles would be performed to see the children of Israel delivered (Exodus 4:19-23). Moses was set. And yet, Exodus 4:24 tells us that when he and his family were on their way to Egypt, God became so angry with Moses that He sought to kill him. What happened between verses 23 and 24?

God had instructed Moses to go back to Egypt to lead His people out of slavery and to remind them how to walk in the ways of the Lord. This meant that they would have to reinstitute the act of circumcision. Moses agreed to take the message to the people but did not put it into practice in his home first. Verse 25 says that Moses' wife Zipporah took a sharp stone, circumcised their son, cast the foreskin at Moses' feet and said, "Surely you are a husband of blood to me!" Zipporah stepped in to do what God had told Moses to do, and she did so with a horrible attitude. Without reading too much into the text, it seems to me that Moses had lost control of his family. Perhaps when he first introduced the plan for circumcision Zipporah didn't like the idea. Instead of being strong in leadership, explaining the importance of obedience in the act of circumcision, Moses gave in and chose disobedience because it was the road of least resistance . . . at least he thought it was. God resisted violently.

Verse 26 tells us that God then let Moses go, which sounds like a good thing because He didn't kill Moses. However, I believe that God stepped out of the picture because Zipporah stepped in. God was dealing with Moses when Zipporah thought she could do a better job. So, God let her do her thing. Just a side note here about dealing with sin in your spouse's life: If you step in where God is trying to correct and discipline, He will let you, but you will never succeed in correcting your spouse. Only

God can change a heart, so don't try to do His job for Him.

The saddest part of this story comes later in Exodus 18, after all of the plagues, the Passover, the miraculous deliverance from slavery and the parting of the Red Sea. After all of these miracles, Jethro (Moses' father-in-law) came to Moses with Zipporah and his two sons. This means that somewhere along the way, Moses had sent his family back to Midian to live with his in-laws. The dispute between Moses and Zipporah had become so intense and distracting that Moses had given up on leading them and sent them away.

Moses' two sons missed out on the most spectacular portion of his ministry, the abounding miracles and presence of God. When the other boys in camp would sit around the fire and remember when God turned the sea to blood and all of Egypt was plagued with frogs, Moses' boys sat silent. Their parents were separated during that time, and they missed out. Their faith wasn't stretched as the Angel of Death passed by their door on Passover night. They couldn't say that they had walked on the dry bottom of the Red Sea surrounded by walls of water suspended by the very hand of God.

If you have ever wondered why Moses' sons did not join the family business in leading Israel after their father's death, it is because Moses was strong in leading Israel but not strong in leading his family. When Moses sent the twelve spies to check out the Promised Land, only two, Joshua and Caleb, came back with reports of God's ability to overcome the giants. There should have been four. Moses' sons should have been there living out the faith they had inherited from their father. They should have come back ready to take on the Philistines and the Ammonites and the Moabites and whoever else stood in their way because their dad had shown them the invincible power of God. Who knows how his sons' lives could have been different, if only.

You have a choice. You can choose to be strong, strong in spirit and in prayer and in leadership, embarking on great journeys of faith. Your family will be right behind you, learning and participating in the adventure. They will go on to even greater things because you inspired them. Or, you can choose to be passive in your walk with Christ and passive in leading your family. Undoubtedly you will struggle with the negative effect it will have on their character, but it might not be until eternity that you see all that they missed out on because of your weakness. Either way, your wife and children will likely come to know God the way you lead them to know Him. Leadership is influence. What mark do you want to leave?

CHAPTER 4

You're the Man

Bill was thrilled about his new job as marketing director for a major architectural firm. He had been out of work for a few months and was ready to jump in head first to remind the world what he was made of. His supervisor, Jerry, met him at the door on his first day to welcome him and show him around the office.

After taking the grand tour and meeting about 50 people whose names he had already forgotten, Bill settled in behind his desk as Jerry continued the orientation. "Bill," Jerry said, "we are so excited that you have joined our organization. From what I know of your work ethic and experience, you are a perfect fit. We are all counting on you to complete our team and make us even more successful than we already are."

"I'm thrilled to be here, Jerry. I will give you 100 percent, and together we will conquer the architectural world."

"Well, I am so glad to hear you say that. Listen, my office is just down the hall. Don't hesitate to knock on my door if you have any questions." With that last comment, Jerry got up, left the office, closing the door behind him on a very confused Bill.

"*Wait a minute,*" Bill thought, "*is that all the training I'm going to get? I've been hired as the marketing director; and I know this is an architectural firm, but beyond that, I am not sure what they want from me.*" He looked around the office, sparsely decorated. In the drawers, there were only office supplies and empty file folders. On his desk, a phone and computer sat waiting to be operated. But who should he call? What project should he work on?

After contemplating for a few minutes, Bill set out to find Jerry and take him up on his offer to answer some questions. Rapping on the door gently, Bill poked his head in to find Jerry already buried in work. "Oh, Bill," Jerry looked up, "come on in. What can I do for you?"

"Well," Bill began, "I need a little direction. Can you fill in a few details on what my job description entails?"

Jerry furrowed his brow and asked, "What do you mean 'details'? You are the marketing director of a major architectural firm."

"Yes, this I know," Bill grinned. "But in order for me to really excel, I would like to know a little about what the last person in my position did and what the company now expects from its new marketing director."

Jerry leaned back in his chair, stunned that his new star employee would ask such questions. "Bill, if you don't know what is expected of you here, I am not going to tell you. You should have thought of that before you took on this job . . . "

Does your marriage sometimes feel like this? I'm sure you've heard the "if you don't know, I'm not going to tell you" comment before! Do you feel like you jumped in enthusiastically only to find out that your wife has some significant needs and high expectations of you, but she is not telling you what they are? Women are notorious for mistaking men for mind readers and then getting angry when they fail to read their minds. Just as Bill has no chance of thriving in a position where the expectations are not outlined, neither can you expect to be a good husband when you don't know what your wife needs from you.

God has designed man to be able to meet his wife's needs. Of course, there are some needs that only God can meet, and you should never try to meet those. For example, her need for a redeemed and sanctified heart can only be met by Jesus and the Holy Spirit. You are not her Savior. However, in His master design of man and woman, God has equipped each with skills and traits that can satisfy many of their spouse's needs. Still, if you don't know what those needs are, you can't very well fill them.

Though not all women are exactly alike, they are all made by the same God who wired them all the same way. If you think you can trade your wife in for a newer model and be rid of the problems you have in marriage, think again. They are all the same under the hood!

Women's needs are primarily emotional. They are vulnerable creatures who crave intimacy. Men are not primarily emotional. We are physical, and our idea of intimacy has more to do with body contact than feelings. In order to be the godly husband that your wife needs, you will have to die to the flesh you have become comfortable wallowing in.

There is a danger in unmet needs. As a man, if you are not respected in your home and if your wife is not meeting your sexual needs, the lady that sits at the next desk who thinks the world of you and seems very willing to put out becomes a treacherous enticement. Women have affairs too, and for similar reasons. An unfaithful wife is looking for a man who will meet the needs that her husband is not meeting at home.

God once told me that He wanted to help me list my priorities. I thought that was a good idea, so I got out a piece of paper, numbered it one through three and wrote "God" by number one. Immediately I heard the Father say, "I didn't tell you to write that."

"Yes, God, I know you didn't say to write that, but I know that it is the right answer. I mean, in case You have forgotten, I've studied this and even preached on it. Everyone's list of priorities should read: God, family, work."

Again, He said, "I did not tell you to write that."

"Fine," I said as I crumpled it up and threw it away. I got another sheet and sat to wait on God. He spoke clearly to me and said, "Write number one." And I wrote number one. "Now," He said, "write Debbie."

I was so confused. "But God, You are supposed to be first in my life. I love You and want to serve You."

His answer struck me: "If you love me and want to serve me, obey me. Make Debbie first in your life. If she is first, then I know I will be first."

Your wife must take first priority in your life. You need a

demotion, and she needs a promotion. If you make that one change, you will see marked improvement in your marriage. When she knows she is first in your life, her greatest need is met: her need for security. Above all else, women crave security, and you have been equipped to make her secure. You are the man God has chosen to meet this need in her life.

Be the Man for Life

When a woman senses that you are not totally committed to her, she feels extremely insecure. It is quite unsettling for her to think that her husband might pack up any day and leave her. Remember, women are emotional beings, so your actions and words are always translated by her heart. A secure future with her husband communicates love, acceptance and belonging.

If your wife questions your loyalty to her, you may have given her good reason to doubt you. Her interpretation of your intentions may have come from one of those verbal threats you've been known to blast at her: "One of these days I am going to walk out that door and never come back!" Whether or not you mean it, her fear and insecurity will be born out of your words.

Other times though, it might be less clear to you where she gets her fear of abandonment. One possibility might be other men in her life – her father, past relationships or even close friends. Has she been abandoned before? If so, it was probably very traumatic for her. To protect herself from such pain breaking her again, she walked into marriage expecting you to leave her. And because you didn't realize she felt insecure about your future together, you have never done anything to stabilize her concern.

Your wife needs to know that you are committed to nourish and cherish her to full maturity. Jesus is committed to us, His bride, in this way. He works daily, nourishing and cherishing our hearts. Nourishment brings full maturity. Cherishing protects that which is maturing. As believers, we know that we will never be fully mature until we see Jesus face-to-face. Thus, that is the timeline you are committed to in marriage. Daily, until death separates you, you should be nourishing and cherishing your bride.

God is also committed to your wife, and He is actually the One who makes her more like Christ. What He plants in her, you are to cultivate. God will work in her with or without your cooperation, but you cripple her growth process when you don't agree with Him. If God wants to teach her to trust Him more but you are completely untrustworthy, she will struggle with believing that she should really trust God. However, when you give her a sense of security, trusting God is more feasible because you have shown her that faith doesn't disappoint.

Jesus promised us that He would never leave us or forsake us (Hebrews 13:5). That floods my heart with peace and confidence. Your heart for your wife must correspond with Jesus' heart for you. She needs the same confidence from you that you have from Jesus.

You are the man God has given her for life to meet her greatest need for security. Be that man . . . for life. Verbally affirm your commitment to her and then follow up your words with actions that validate her trust in you. Such security will fill your wife with peace and hope for the future.

Be the Man Who Provides

A man, a strong man, takes responsibility. When my son, Josh, went to college, he took responsibility for himself. Although I was still helping him financially, he managed his time and money well, paid his bills and made good grades. When he graduated, he got a job and began providing for himself. Not much later, he got married and began taking care of his wife. Josh chose to be a man when he took responsibility. Until he was out on his own, taking responsibility for his own life, he was still a boy. Age, size, marital status, fatherhood, wealth . . . don't make a boy a man. Taking responsibility makes him a man.

Women need security. God made MAN to meet that need in her life; a boy can't do a man's job. An immature, irresponsible boy, no matter how old he is, can never meet the need for security in a woman's life because he won't step up and take responsibility. Because I believe in traditional roles for men and women, I want to challenge you to take the lead in providng for your family. That doesn't mean that your wife can't work, but it does mean that her paycheck should not be the one that your family relies on to buy the groceries, make the car payment and pay the electric bill.

Not only should you make the money for your family's provision, but you should handle the money responsibly. When bills come in, pay them on time. A due date of the 15th does not mean mail it on the 15th. Set a budget and live by it, and make your family live by it as well. Explain to them that the budget dictates how you live today and makes life tomorrow possible, as well. Put money away so that you can handle emergencies when they come up. Proverbs says that foolish people live on their whole income, but the wise man saves (Proverbs 6:6-11).

By taking the role of provider in your home, you command respect. Your children will recognize you as the head and thus will honor you as head. If you always send them to their mother when they ask for money, you rob yourself of the authority you need to lead the home. You have given them the picture that their mother is the head of the home. One day, you could very well hear your son in the front yard saying to his friends, "When I grow up, I want to be a real man, like Mom."

Your wife should not to be the head of your home; you should. This was God's plan from the beginning. Sin made that difficult because now we would rather give into our flesh and be irresponsible. If you continue to give into that spirit, your wife will sink further and further into anxiety, and your marriage will fall further and further away from the heights of potential that God planned for it to reach.

The eighth verse of 1 Timothy 5 says:

But if anyone does not provide for his own, and especially for those of his household, he has denied the faith and is worse than an unbeliever.

Ouch. Those are strong words. Because God intended for man to meet the needs of His family, He takes it very seriously when a man who claims to love Him doesn't do it.

Woman was the crown of God's creation. He made her beautiful and fragile. She mirrors His emotional side, and in His perfect plan He ordained security for her through us. When you provide for her, you are not just securing a roof over her head and food in her stomach, you are telling her that she is valuable to you. When she knows that you will dig ditches for her in order to provide, she knows you have died to yourself and are putting her first. Your wife's emotional stability is directly linked to your dependability. Your provision makes her an emotional rock, unshakable and satisfied.

A selfless, sacrificial servant makes a woman secure. A selfish, lazy sluggard makes a woman insecure. You represent God to your wife. What is she learning from your portrayal?

Be the Man in the Face of Danger

I taught Debbie how to shoot a gun. She's a pretty good shot too! Once she knew how to handle the gun, I taught her what to do if a man ever breaks into our home: Boom! Boom! "What do you want?" Shoot first, ask later. Anyone breaking into a house with the intent to harm that family has no business being there.

Debbie needs to be secure, emotionally, financially and physically as well. Not only does she need to know she is safe, she also needs to know her kids are safe. My family knows to lock the doors to the house even if they are at home. My wife and daughter know not to be alone in dangerous parts of town. My sons know how to fight to protect themselves. My daughter knows that she shouldn't get herself in a precarious situation with a boy, no matter how cute he is.

How did my family get to be so wise and cautious? I taught them. As their leader, I have instructed them on the importance of being watchful and guarded. When I am with them, I make sure they are safe; when I am not with them, I know they are armed with wisdom and common sense.

My life was pretty rough before I met Jesus. I threw my share of fists . . . I ate my share of fists, too. I remember one time getting beat up really bad. It was five against two, and those were the toughest two guys I have ever met! Anyway, when my boys were old enough, I not only taught them how to fight, but when to fight. Waging war on their peers would not earn them respect but defending themselves would. And more than that, shielding the women in their lives from danger would make them heroes.

To my last breath, I will protect my family. But keeping my family out of the hospital is not the only way I protect them. Satan's weapons can hurt them much worse than a broken bone. It is vital that I make my family aware of the dangers lurking, tempting them away from godliness. When I set limits on what kind of music my children are allowed to listen to, I explain why. We look together in the Bible where it talks about the importance of filling your mind with virtuous, praiseworthy thoughts (Philippians 4:8). When I refused to let my daughter date at age 13, I read the verse with her that exhorts: "Do not stir up nor awaken love/Until it pleases" (Song of Solomon 2:7). By making the Bible the standard in our home for decision-making, I equip my children with wisdom that will protect them for life.

My wife knows she is safe, and she knows her children are safe because she has a husband who is committed to their security. Above all, we trust God to watch out for our family. It may seem illogical to say we trust God when we live so cautiously, but it's not. I trust God to provide for me, but I still work. In the same way, I trust God to protect me; but I still lock my doors. God's provision and security often come through my job and because of my locked door. I partner with God in protecting my family by teaching them safety skills and insisting that they use them.

You Are the Man

There has been a lot of chatter in the church lately about the "Jezebel spirit." While this is a valid threat to the body of Christ, there is another spirit present that is enabling the Jezebel spirit: the Ahab spirit. Ahab was the king of Israel who conquered more land than anyone except for Solomon. This mighty conqueror ruled his kingdom; but when he came home, he answered to Jezebel. Jezebel ruled the castle. We can see the extent of her power and control in 1 Kings 21.

Ahab returned to Samaria after great conquests and decided that he wanted the vineyard adjacent to the palace. He approached the owner, Naboth, and promised a fair trade for the vineyard. Naboth refused the king. This greatly upset Ahab; and he went home, crawled in bed and sucked his thumb. When Jezebel found him and learned of his sorrow, she consoled him with compliments . . . and then she took control. Jezebel arranged a feast for Naboth, complete with false witnesses instructed to accuse Naboth of blasphemy. When the lies were spread, Naboth was taken out of the city and stoned. Ahab got his vineyard. Jezebel sat as reigning queen over her husband.

There is an Ahab spirit in families enabling women to step up and replace their husbands as the head of the home. These women suffer from an unmet need for security. They don't go out and have affairs; they just usurp power and wield it to build a false sense of security, which they think is better than no security at all. They have Ahabs who rule the business world but avoid home life. They believe they have to take control or else their family will break down. Women take motherhood seriously, and when there is no husband willing to step up and take responsibility, they will do whatever it takes to care for the children. Her ascension to the head of the family will devastate her and her children. She was not meant to play that part; she is not equipped. You are the only one in their lives who can secure them. You are the man.

God created you to be a leader. Don't be intimidated by that role; seize the opportunity to fulfill your purpose in life to be a strong husband and father. Ahab led two lives: a conquering lifestyle in the professional world and a defeated lifestyle in the home. His wife succeeded though in stealing his glory and legacy. It is not by coincidence that her name is still famous today while most people ask, "Ahab? Never heard of him."

After reading this chapter, do you recognize that there could be a spirit of insecurity attacking your wife? Do you see some practical ways that you can pick up responsibility so that her greatest need can be met? You will be surprised how quickly your commitment to her emotional, financial and physical well-being will change her outlook toward life and toward you.

Don't drive your wife to anxiety and panic because of insecurity. And don't enable her to become a Jezebel either. Be the strong man she needs every day, for life.

70

CHAPTER 5

Dive into the Deep

Over and over in this book, I have reiterated that men and women are different. From the beginning, Debbie and I have tried to convince you that diversity between genders is a good thing for marriage. Sometimes, however, it may seem like a bad thing. Like when you are trying to watch the game and she is rambling on and on about what Susie said to Maggie in church that morning. Or like when Phil and Linda invite you over to their house Friday night for fondue and Scrabble and she says yes! Or like when you are wrestling with the kids in the floor and she gets annoyed that you got them "all riled up just before bedtime." In those moments, you probably don't treasure the contrast in your wife.

Why can't women be more like men? Well, I don't think we even want to answer that one. Men agree that women are magnificent creatures . . . even if their behavior is annoying sometimes. They are beautiful and soft and warm. We love to be with them, when they are not being too weird that is.

In Genesis 2, when God first made Eve, what do you think was running through Adam's mind? He had been in a deep sleep, deep enough not to feel God cut a rib out of his side and sew him back up. When he woke up, he yawned, stretched, scratched and then turned around, coming face-to-face with the most glorious sight he had ever seen. There she stood, naked and unashamed, feminine grace in all her splendor. You remember how you felt on your wedding night . . . well magnify that by like a million, and maybe you can imagine Adam's delight.

Before sin entered their relationship, Adam and Eve were able to celebrate one another's uniqueness without getting irritated or angry. He loved her knack for decorating, and she loved his playfulness. He cherished her ability to tunnel into his heart, and she treasured the times when he would hold her close as they gazed at the stars together. However, after the fruit and serpent incident, neither related to the other perfectly any more. Her promptings became nagging, and his silence became painful.

When God gave Eve to Adam, he wanted the two of them to become one, not just one flesh, but one spirit. They were created for intimacy. God knew that Adam had been lonely, and He created Eve with a longing for companionship as well. If they didn't come together to meet one another's needs, both would be miserable.

For most men, "intimacy" is a scary word. It paints pictures of cry-fests and sappy poetry. We are afraid that if we give into this intimacy thing, we will start renting chick-flicks and sniffling through Hallmark commercials. A man's man does not tear up over a puppy wrapped in a bow. It just should not be.

Well, from one man's man to another, take heart! Intimacy will not weaken or cheapen your manhood. It will only strengthen your marriage. God's plan from the beginning was that you become one spirit with your wife, and that involves going deeper with her on a heart level. She wants to know the you that lies below the tough exterior: your passions, your dreams, your disappointments and your fears. Don't worry. She will not love you any less if she finds out that you were once fired for incompetence or that you are afraid of looking like a wimp in front of your buddies. Women are strange like that. The more they know about you, good or bad, the more they are drawn to you. I think that happens because she has a need for intimacy that is met when you reveal your heart to her, and thus she feels closer to you because you met that need. Your wife wants to know you, and she wants you to know her. While you may never fully understand her, you can know her intimately.

She Wants Your Affection

It is no surprise to men that our second greatest need is sex. We are reminded daily, hourly, of our need for sex. Your wife may not understand it, but don't worry because Debbie is going to explain that to her later on in the book.

I think God gave us a hunger for sex so that we would stay committed to our wives. Imagine if men had no sex drive. They would go hunting together, gather around the fire at night, gnawing their latest kill, all scratching their heads thinking, "Hmmm, I feel like there is somewhere I was supposed to be tonight." Meanwhile, Ma would be sitting at home, tapping her foot, rolling her eyes and sighing, "That numskull. He forgot us again. Guess I'm going to have to go out to the deer lease and drag him back!" That sounds funny because it would never happen. No matter how manly our day was, hunting or conquering, we are driven back to our wives because there is an intense need that only she can meet. Thank God for sex drive!

Women don't need sex like we do, but they do need affection. You might be thinking, "What's the difference? Sex, affection, same thing, right?" Wrong. I once heard about a survey that asked women to rate their needs. Sex didn't even come in the top ten. It even rated lower than gardening! Apparently fresh basil is more important to a woman than sex. However, she craves affection.

So, if sex isn't affection, then what in the world is affection? Allow me to give you a few examples: Holding her hand, caressing her, putting your arm around her waist, embracing her. Your wife knows that when you reach out to touch her, you want to have sex with her. She is not stupid. In fact, over the years, she has probably developed a radar that goes off when you enter the room: "Pervert alert! Pervert alert!" She has turned cold to your need for sex because you have ignored her need for affection. How do you think your wife would respond if you sat next to her on the couch, put your arms around her, pulled her close and cuddled with her for an hour . . . and then didn't have sex with her? She would be stunned, but she would also be fulfilled.

Men, I want to tell you that when you go out of your way to gratify her need for affection, she will be much more willing to gratify your need for sex. Most of the time we think, "I'm going to turn on the charm tonight. She won't be able to resist me. I'll unbutton my shirt, slip on a gold chain, douse myself with a little aftershave, and she will be all over me like mustard on a hot dog!" Well, if you haven't noticed by now, no matter how suave your strut is, she is not very impressed. Don't get me wrong, I am sure you are magnificent, chest hair and all, but you are not irresistible. Do you know what is irresistible to a woman? Affection. Making out on the couch without dragging her to the bedroom is a major turn on to her.

Another side bonus to becoming more affectionate might be that you discover that you like non-sexual touch. Don't fight it. I love to be held by my wife. Now, I don't like to be held by my friend Brady, but I love it when Debbie holds me. Never do I need a hug from my golfing buddies, but getting a hug from Debbie thrills me. I still love sex; I am a man. But my wife's touch has opened up a whole new world that generates energy and vitality in our alone time.

I have also discovered that romance goes hand-in-hand with affection. When I am affectionate with my wife, I am telling her that I love her company more than her body. When I turn on the romance, I am telling her that I crave her company more than her body.

Has your wife ever complained that you are not romantic? Maybe you think that you are not creative enough to be romantic. The trick to romance is not grand ideas, expensive taste or a knack for writing ballads. The trick to romance is planning ahead. Ask your wife on Tuesday if you can take her on a date on Friday. When Friday rolls around, have the evening already planned out. Send her flowers or a card on a day when you are not in trouble. Leave a note in the drawer for her to find when she is cooking. Surprising her with romance tells her that she is on your mind even when she is not with you.

Be aware though, you can't be very romantic if you are not a good financial manager. Putting a $40 bouquet of flowers on the nearly maxed out credit card fails to communicate romance. Instead, the gesture knocks the legs out from under her ability to trust you to provide for her. Remember, security is her number one need. If your budget is tight, pick a bouquet of wild flowers on your way home from work instead of charging it. She will be just as touched, and you will not shake her trust in your ability to take care of her.

There is one major road block to affection, romance and intimacy that cannot be ignored or sidestepped, and that is impurity. You will never be drawn to your wife and she will never be drawn to you if you are a slave to pornography. The women you lust after and fantasize about form an unrealistic and unhealthy measuring stick in your mind that you constantly use to measure your wife.

Think of the time and mental energy that are wasted on the addiction to pornography. Even if an addiction is not all consuming, these movies and magazines will work against a wife not for her. Consider this: If your wife were the only woman on earth, you would probably kill to have sex with her. It's true, isn't it? Why then is she not satisfying you now? Stop comparing her to other women, and she will gratify every sexual need you have.

A friend of mine once recommended a movie to Debbie and me. He told us it was really good, but it did have one sex scene in it. Debbie and I are affected differently by movies. I can see someone's head blown up in slow motion and not be bothered, but Debbie would have nightmares for a week. Debbie can watch a love scene and think of me. I, on the other hand, would be trapped and tempted by lust in watching that same scene. Because of our weaknesses, we have set boundaries on what we will watch. I don't ask her to watch violence, and she doesn't ask me to watch sensuality. In respecting one another's convictions, we promote holiness in our marriage and push the other toward godliness.

When our friend asked if we wanted to see the movie with the sex scene, I turned it down. Later, Debbie asked me if there were any part of me that wished I could see that scene. "Absolutely not," I told her. "It was too hard to get free from that bondage the first time. I don't want to be a slave again." It is hell to be with the most beautiful woman and to be thinking about someone else. Brothers, whatever it takes to get free from the impurity that plagues your mind, do it. The empty pleasures of pornography are nothing compared to the splendor that awaits you in the arms of your wife.

Do you dream of a more fulfilling sex life? Die to your desires in order to fulfill hers. I promise, when you do, she will reciprocate and surprise you. She will want you and come after you, and you won't even need that gold chain.

Connecting the Wires

Men come emotionally unattached. We are like those toys that come with a hundred parts that you have to put together for your kids on Christmas Eve. Man's approach to the heart is to ignore the instructions and to never use all the parts! And just like the toys, we end up flawed but functional. Women, on the other hand, come completely assembled emotionally. They are totally connected to their feelings and usually to everyone else's as well.

Why is this important to you? Because communication is another of women's greatest needs. When conversing with you, they don't just want the game highlights; they want the play-by-play and the after game interviews as well. For you newly married guys, you may just be discovering this about your wife. Most likely, she is not satisfied with, "My day was fine." No, she wants to know, "What did you do? Why did you do that? What were you wearing when you did that?" Honestly, she will probably not be satisfied until you explain: "At 6:32 a.m. I opened my eyes. I had a bit of a headache which I assume is linked to some stressful situations at work. I think I feel stressed because . . . " That's right, she wants to know it all. Now, she is not being nosy; she is looking for you to meet her need. She cannot be satisfied with a head-to-head connection with you; she wants a heart-to-heart.

The problem is that men don't know how to connect heart-to-heart. We don't even know such a connection is possible. That is why God gives us wives. If you will let her, she will connect those wires that were neglected when you were assembled. You may not realize it, but you have all the necessary parts to communicate with your wife emotionally. You just don't know how they all work.

When your wife begins asking questions about your past, she will go beyond who, what, when and where. Those questions we can generally handle. It gets confusing when she jumps into the how and why. For example, the first time you tell her that your father abandoned you at age six, her first question might be, "Oh, and how did you feel about that?" You, of course, will see her mouth moving and even hear sounds emitting from her lips, but you will have no idea what she is asking. Feelings do not come naturally to men, thus talking with your wife in *emotion-ese* will be like speaking a foreign language.

As unfamiliar as it is to you, your wife still needs you to connect with her, and you are committed to meeting her needs. So let her help you. Think of her as your interpreter and language teacher. The next time she asks you about feelings, go with her. She will pick up one of your wires and say, "See this? This is when your father left you."

"Yes," you will say, "I see that."

Picking up another wire, she'll ask, "Now, see this? This is how that made you feel."

"Whoa, what is that? I've never seen that before."

"And when you put them together," as she crosses the live wires . . . bzzzzz.

"Ouch! That hurts," you cry.

"Exactly. That is what it felt like when your father left you." You see, the feelings are there, you just don't know how to connect with them.

There will always be times when your differences will make interaction difficult. If you ask when dinner will be ready and she says, "I just have to put the rolls in," don't get frustrated. Even though her reply didn't actually answer your question, don't throw the towel in. Calmly ask how long rolls take to cook, and then you will know for the next time. More importantly, move past those petty differences and onto more important things. When dinner is on the table, ask her questions that will draw her heart out, and then respond to her inquiries with the detail she desires. I have gotten in the habit of outlining my conversations with people throughout the day so that I can better communicate with my wife at the end of the day. Since I know she will want details, I mentally gather them and save them for her. This may sound like a hassle, but she is worth it to me.

Why, you ask, would you want to learn how to feel or communicate if you've gotten along for so many years without it? Well, remember that women mirror God's emotional side. He is emotional like women are, except without sin. You will not truly know Him until you can communicate with Him in the language of His heart, feelings. When I became a better communicator with Debbie, my prayer life intensified. When I dove into the depth of her feelings, I learned how to dive deeply into the passionate heart of God, too. He became more real to me because I could finally speak the language of His heart.

Dig deeper into your wife's heart. Allow her to explore the

depth of yours as well. You can truly connect with her. There will come a time when you get a buzz off of hearing her share her heart. When her need for communication is met, you will look back and realize that intimacy is the gravity that is pulling your hearts together, joining your spirits and making you one.

There's Always Hope

Men, when I first got married, I was clueless. I thought married life would be my old carefree life of leisure with the added bonuses of a housekeeper, home-cooked meals and regular sex. There were days when I would hardly see my wife because I would busy myself with work or play or both. I remember rolling my eyes at my precious bride because she seemed so apprehensive and nervous about everything. Even when she tried to find common ground and enter my world of sports, I would belittle her athletic ability because in my eyes, she was only as good as a girl could be. Honestly, in high school, Debbie was a better athlete than I was! Early on, my pride wouldn't let me recognize that though. She would go play golf with me, fish with me, and she even tried scuba diving once. I just couldn't see what a blessing she was to me. Like I said, I was clueless.

Debbie, on the other hand, was a saint. She put up with my shenanigans without complaining or nagging. Instead of trying to change me, she went to God. To this day there is a room in our house that serves as her refuge; I don't even know where it is! But when I am acting up, she goes there and talks to God about me. I am the husband I am today because Debbie has prayed for me fervently and faithfully. God loves my wife even more than I do, and when she goes to Him with my selfish ways, He always steps in to straighten me out.

Maybe you are reading this book as an answer to the prayers of your faithful wife. Maybe you are the interceding one in your marriage, crying out to God for help and healing. Whatever your circumstance, the blessed marriage is within your reach! You saw where I came from . . . nothing is impossible with God!

We serve a God of mercy who forgives us for our boneheaded ways and then steps beyond pardon to change us from the inside out. His plan for you is that you turn into Jesus. Jesus was the ultimate man, strong yet tender, bold yet compassionate. Nothing He set out to accomplish failed. He loved passionately and unconditionally, gave Himself sacrificially and trusted the Father wholly. He lived a life of example and then told us to follow Him. The roadmap to blessing in your marriage lies in the pages of Matthew, Mark, Luke and John. If you don't know how to change, start reading there, observing the ways of Christ and then imitating them in your home. Walk in Jesus' footsteps, deny yourself and take up your cross daily. In Christ, death does not lead to defeat. The glorious truth we saw three days after the crucifixion is that for Jesus and His followers, victorious life always springs forth from death.

CHAPTER 6

The King of the Castle

A few years into our marriage, Robert and I were having dinner with a pastor and his wife. Even though we deeply loved each other, our immaturity caused me to be frustrated and annoyed with Robert frequently. From this dissatisfaction in my heart, I slammed my husband's pride in front of our hosts. Trying to be funny and desiring acceptance from this couple, I aired one of my private grievances publicly.

Immediately, I knew I had made a huge mistake. Knowing glances shot across the table; courteous laughs confirmed my humiliation as the knot in my stomach hardened. Worst of all, the look on Robert's face showed his devastation. My own conscience convicted me . . . I had slandered my husband in order to make myself look and feel better.

Later, as I was helping the pastor's wife in the kitchen, she offered words of counsel that changed my approach toward my husband. Tenderly she said, "Debbie, every man should be king in his own home. If Robert isn't a king in your home, then where will he be king?"

Her wise admonishment rang true in my heart. As unhappy as I was in my marriage, deep down I knew that Robert needed to be honored and respected. What I didn't know was that honor was the key to my husband's heart. Forget the old adage that promises, "The way to a man's heart is through his stomach." My whole menu repertoire could fit on a post-it note, so I would have little hope in winning my man's heart if that saying were true! But I do have my husband's heart because honor became the magnet that has drawn Robert toward me consistently for twenty-six years.

You may be thinking, "Yeah Debbie, that is fine for you. Robert is a good husband, deserving of respect. I'm married to an oaf who treats me horribly. You can't expect me to honor that!" Sweet sister, no man is perfect, and none other than Jesus consistently earns respect. However your husband acts, it is your privilege and responsibility to respond to him with honor.

Jesus was a man, and as such He was affected by honor and respect. In Matthew 13, we learn that after Jesus already had been ministering throughout Judea, He went back to His own country and to His own people. He taught in the synagogue with great wisdom, so remarkably in fact that the people of Nazareth began to question His ability. How could Jesus, the carpenter's son, speak with such authority? These people, His friends, family and neighbors, discredited His ministry. Jesus responded:

> *"Only in his hometown and in his own*
> *house is a prophet without honor."*
> *(Matthew 13:57, NIV)*

Even Jesus, the only perfect man ever to walk the earth, was scorned by his family and friends, proving that familiarity breeds contempt. As a result, Matthew 13:58 tells us that, "He did not do many mighty works there because of their unbelief."

I find it amazing that Jesus, the Word of God who spoke the world into existence and came to earth in human form, was hindered by unbelief. Surely He did not lack the ability to do miracles, but He did lack the means. God always works through faith, thus the unbelief of those closest to Jesus caused them to miss out on the wonders of God. Their lack of faith was evident in their refusal to honor Jesus. This suggests to me that there is power in honoring! If their refusal to honor Jesus became a hindrance to Him, could our refusal to honor our husbands be a hindrance to them as well? If we choose to honor our husbands, might we be releasing them to do incredible things?

My journey as a wife and my testimony of God's gracious patience in teaching me how to be a wife say, "Yes!" Ephesians 5:33 tells wives to respect and honor their husbands. God does not give us impossible tasks to obey just so He can watch us squirm. He knows how our husbands are wired because He is the One who wired them. One way males image God is the way they respond to honor. The respect we are commanded to give to our husbands is the first step we can take toward the blessed marriage God has called us to experience. I guarantee that you will be amazed at the change in your husband when you begin to honor him.

Learning to Honor

According to *Nelson's Illustrated Bible Dictionary*, the

word "honor" is synonymous with "esteem" and "respect."[1] *The International Standard Bible Encyclopedia* explains that "respect" is a verb insinuating "to lift up the face."[2] I love this definition because it implies that my respectful approach toward my husband can turn his downcast face upward. God has given me this amazing ability to encourage and strengthen Robert. When he is fearful or ashamed, God will use my reverent attitude toward him to lift his head.

According to the *McClintock and Strong Encyclopedia,* " . . . honor rests on the judgment of the thinking."[3] In other words, true honor begins in the mind and is formed by our responses to our husbands' actions. Allow me to paint two common scenarios to help illustrate my point.

A foursome of tennis league ladies sits in an upscale restaurant sipping drinks and ordering off a menu of scandalously high-priced entrees. Adorned with diamonds and the latest Nike fashion, each attempts to trump the other with tales of their newest furniture purchases or latest world travels. Soon, the topic of conversation drifts to the men in their lives. Instead of praising and acknowledging their husbands' hard work that makes their lives of luxury possible, they proceed in bashing them for how insensitive or unattractive or absent they are.

Just up the road, four other women gather in a break room for coffee and chit-chat. It doesn't take long before one of them tells an embarrassing tale of her husband's recent failure at work. Attempting to top that story, another tells of her husband's deficiencies; and the competition goes around the table . . . whose husband is the worst? Even the good ones are torn apart like shark bait!

When we as wives choose to criticize our husbands' every move, we rob them of the respect they need to be successful. In his book *Marriage on the Rock,* Jimmy Evans explains that honor is man's number one need.[4] In fact, it is so dominant that men will gravitate to wherever that need is met. If they are praised on the golf course, they will play golf every weekend. If they are respected at work, they will work extra long hours. If they are honored at the local coffee shop by the waitress who never lets his cup run dry, he will frequent that shop every morning. He is *your* husband; don't allow his needs to be met by someone else.

If you see how your disrespectful attitude is harming your marriage and holding your husband back from becoming the man God wants him to be, you know that you need to change. But how? Again, an honoring attitude begins with an honoring heart. You must recognize that your husband deserves honor, first because of his position, second because of his performance, and third because your providential honoring can release a creative power in your husband's life.

First, you must recognize that your husband was a gift to you from God and is the head of your household. Presidents and kings receive honor just because they are in a position of honor. God wants to be praised because He is God, not just because He does good things. In the same manner, your husband has been placed in a position of honor in your home. That demands respect. He may not be a president, a king or Jesus; but his status in your home is deserving of honor.

Second, your husband deserves respect for his hard work. Athletes compete for a gold medal. Students strive for the distinction of valedictorian. Writers long for the recognition of a Nobel Prize. It is human nature to desire praise for a job well done. Any man who goes to work every day is worthy of honor in his home. He doesn't have to be employee of the month or climb the corporate ladder to earn his family's respect. The very act of going day after day to a job where he is likely under-appreciated for work he doesn't enjoy just so that he can provide for his family is worthy of tremendous praise. Your grateful heart will motivate your husband to work hard every day because he is proud of what he is accomplishing for his family.

Finally, we should honor our husbands because of the men they can become. I call this providential honor because it speaks of divine guidance. God has planted seeds of greatness in your husband that must be tended and cultivated to reach maturity. By respecting his potential, you create a womb for his dreams to grow and come to life in. When I learned to honor Robert in this way, my heart toward him completely changed. It was as though I learned to see him for all he could become in Christ and not just who he was in the moment. Faith for Robert's best was honoring because I was agreeing with God that Robert could become an even greater man of God. In agreeing with God, a creative power was released in our home. I believed the best for Robert, and he grew into that honor. Still today, I honor him for what he will become tomorrow.

Men need respect. They feed off of it. They revel in it. While no man is perfect, all husbands deserve honor for the place they hold in the family as well as for their provision. If your husband is falling short of your expectations, start by praising him for the little things that he does right. I have learned that praising is a hundred times more effective than nagging. He tunes out my whiny voice, but is drawn to my appreciative one.

Honoring in Word and Deed

After receiving encouragement from that pastor's wife to honor Robert as the king of his home, I began wondering what it would look like for me to do this. I read in the Old Testament how Sarah called Abraham "Lord" . . . but such praise sounded out of place in our society today. I remembered that in ancient Japanese culture, women walked behind their husbands, but again, this would just be weird in modern-day America. Once I knew a pastor's wife who always referred to her husband as "Brother Jones." Well, I can't imagine what type of look my husband would give me if I started calling him "Brother Robert" all the time! So then, what does it look like for *me* to honor *my* husband?

Our culture doesn't really provide good examples for us. Instead of truly honoring our leaders, we poke fun at our president. Flimsy attempts at praise come at award banquets or etching names in bricks that are laid into the structure of a building. These are fleeting efforts to honor. Our husbands need more than this.

Matthew 12:34-35 says (emphasis added):

> *"How can you, being evil, speak good things?* For out of the abundance of the heart the mouth speaks. *A good man out of the good treasure of his heart brings forth good things, and an evil man out of the evil treasure brings forth evil things."*

Once you have raised your husband to a seat of honor in your heart, that respect should naturally flow into your words. However, if for years you have criticized, you may have to be more intentional about working praise into your conversation.

Your words have the ability to boost or deflate your husband's potential.

Death and life are in the power of the tongue.
(Proverbs 18:21)

How many times have you said things like, "He is such a jerk," or "He will never change," or "He is just a lazy bum who never helps me"? I admit, there have been many times I uttered words that I wished I could have extracted from the airwaves. When I began to realize the power of my words, both for evil and for good, I made a conscious decision to work with God instead of against Him to release supernatural power through Robert into our marriage and family. Life can flow from your mouth to your husband's heart and even beyond into the atmosphere of your home.

Deciding to speak positive words of encouragement into Robert's life was the easy part; actually doing it every day proved to be more difficult. Before long I realized that if my thoughts toward Robert remained negative, my words would follow suit. For so long, I had been keeping a mental list of all of Robert's faults and mistakes. Every time he messed up, it went on my list. How could I expect to consistently encourage my husband when my only opinions of him were cynical?

One day, I heard a friend explain how she made a practice of praising her husband seven times a day. God prompted me to do the same, but I was pessimistic because I didn't think I could come up with seven things a day to praise Robert for. Had it been seven nags, that would have been no problem!

When my heart finally submitted to God's direction, I tried to praise Robert, but the first few attempts came across awkward and phony. My heart condemned me, "Hypocrite, you don't mean it!" I was right . . . I didn't mean it. My praise was empty flattery not genuine admiration. So, I prayed a prayer something like this, "God, if you want me to praise Robert, You have to help me. Knock the scales off my eyes so that I can see him like You see him." This became my prayer for several weeks and months, and after some time I began to see Robert differently.

The praise of my husband changed from, "It was good that you didn't kick the cat" (said with a sarcastic tone) to "You are such a good provider, and I appreciate how hard you work" (offered with sincere love). Even today I have to refuse to meditate on the negative list. Satan loves to harass me with Robert's faults in an attempt to steal, kill and destroy our marriage. I know his schemes though, and I choose not to believe his lies. I opt for life in my marriage through honoring instead of death to our relationship through dishonoring. Remember:

> *The weapons of our warfare are not carnal but mighty in God for pulling down strongholds, casting down arguments and every high thing that exalts itself against the knowledge of God, bringing every thought into captivity to the obedience of Christ.*
>
> *(2 Corinthians 10:4-5)*

Once my heart, mind and mouth were on the same page, honoring Robert became easier. The next step of respecting him through my actions was a natural one. Proverbs 31:11-12 describes a virtuous wife: "The heart of her husband safely trusts her; So he will have no lack of gain. She does him good and not evil All the days of her life." I learned to honor my husband not just in my heart and with my words but also by following his desires. When Robert was at work, I disciplined our children the way I knew he wanted. When I was shopping, I stuck to the budget he had set for our family. In whatever situation I found myself, I knew Robert wanted his wife to conduct herself with godliness and integrity. I honored his wishes. As his wife, I represent him. Thus I should respect who he is by following his desires.

Have I painted a picture for you of Robert in an angel costume with a glowing halo over his head? You may be thinking that if I can be so generous with praise and so obedient to his desires, he must be a saint! Well, he is not a saint. Robert makes his share of mistakes, but I have learned that even when he messes up, I am still to honor him.

A couple of years ago, Robert and I were counseling a couple. When the wife started inquiring about Robert's faults, I refused to satisfy her curiosity. Annoyed, she asked me why I would cover for Robert. My response to her was, "That is my privilege." I know Robert better than anyone on earth, and I know he is not perfect

. . . but it is my joy not to tell. By keeping his weaknesses between the two of us, I create a safe haven for him to take refuge in. Robert's heart safely trusts mine.

One caution to this advice I give: If your husband is involved in gross sin or abuse, you should not cover for him. It is more loving in these situations to seek help. I only suggest covering his weaknesses and shortcomings when they are not endangering you, him or anyone else.

Ladies, when God created your husbands, He planned great things for them. Your spouse has potential that neither of you are even aware of yet. Who knows? Maybe your husband was meant to lead a great company or invent an amazing product or serve as an anointed minister. Perhaps he was meant to be a great husband, father and grandfather, which are wonderful accomplishments in today's world. Robert has achieved great success as a pastor, author and speaker; but his greatest titles are "devoted husband" and "wonderful father." If no one knew his name, he would still be famous to his family. Your husband may never have a high-profile job; but if he succeeds in his home, he will prove to be great in God's Kingdom.

Be assured that God has planted seeds of greatness in your husband. Your job is to cultivate those seeds through honor and respect. As you praise his hard work today and encourage leaps of faith for tomorrow, you bestow blessings on him that will push him into the greatness God planned for him from the beginning.

When Robert and I were newlyweds, I had an appreciation for the virtue of wisdom. Proverbs 3:13-14 says:

Happy is the man who finds wisdom,
And the man who gains understanding;
For her proceeds are better than the profits of silver,
And her gain than fine gold.

I was so impressed with the value of wisdom that I began asking God to grant Robert wisdom beyond his years. Even more, I began to acknowledge the wise decisions Robert was making as a young man in his twenties. Today, a frequent comment people make about Robert is that he is wise beyond his years. I smile at that, because, while I did not make him wise, I played a part in him becoming wise by agreeing with what God wanted him to become.

Compliments, praise, applause, approval, appreciation . . . your husband needs these from you. It is his greatest emotional need, and he will not be successful unless this need is met. Yes, it will be hard to do at first, but remember what we talked about at the beginning of the book. You are not in a contract relationship with your husband, protecting your rights and limiting your responsibilities. You are in a covenant relationship, meaning that you lay down your rights and you pick up the responsibility to love your husband. Love to your husband is spelled "r-e-s-p-e-c-t."

Order Instead of Chaos

Remember the old television show "All in the Family"? Archie Bunker was certainly the king of his home, but Edith was no queen. She was more like his servant, scurrying around, satisfying his every whim. "Yes, Archie" was the only acceptable response from Edith, and "But, Archie" was seldom tolerated.

Do you think of Edith Bunker when you hear the word "submit"? It is likely that you vowed never to be like Edith, and thus you promised yourself that you would never submit. "Submission" makes us think of "obedience," and that does not exactly appeal to our wills. As women, we want to rule our own lives and our own homes; therefore, we will wage war on anyone or anything that threatens our regime.

Submission is such a hated concept among women because it has been misunderstood. I propose a change of phraseology. Instead of submission, let's use the word "spending." That's less threatening, isn't it? "Spending" makes me think of an infinite balance on my credit cards and limitless possibilities. So, what I suggest to you is that you spend . . . spend your life for your husband. Ok, so I took a turn there. But really, submitting to your husband looks like putting down your rights and demands and instead spending yourself for him.

As wives, we have clear instructions from God's Word to submit. Colossians 3:18 and Ephesians 5:22 both tell us to submit to our husbands as to the Lord. Are you squirming in your seat?

Why would God want us to submit? There is a very simple answer to that question: God wants us to submit because He is a God of order.

When God created the universe, he established order on a planet that was "without form, and void" (Genesis 1:2). He set the sun to rule the day and the moon to rule the night. When He did this, He said that it was good (Genesis 1:17-18). Where chaos had reigned, God spoke harmony.

After Eve ate of the forbidden fruit, God spoke to her and said, "I will greatly multiply your sorrow and your conception; In pain you shall bring forth children; Your desire shall be for your husband, And he shall *rule* over you" (Genesis 3:16, emphasis added). In the same way that God spoke order into day and night, He spoke order into the family.

Have you ever tried to rearrange the pattern of day and night? I have, when I've wanted a few more hours of sleep or a few more hours of day to get things done. But no matter how hard I try, I can't stop the sun or moon from rising. Why not? Because there is a universal order in place.

God's propensity for order can also be seen in the law that He gave to Israel through Moses. There was a specific way He wanted their society to function. Later, God also instructed Moses how to build the tabernacle. He gave him very detailed instructions to follow when constructing His house. After Jesus ascended into heaven and the Holy Spirit came, the church took form. God spoke through the apostles, again instituting order so that the body of Christ could be a functional vessel through which He could work. God is a God of order, always making sense out of what would otherwise be chaos.

God established family order, and He did so because He wanted us to thrive in functional homes that could be instrumental in bringing Him glory. When sin entered the world, so did chaos. Without a respected order, chaos would reign in our homes instead of harmony. Let me ask you, could the turmoil brewing in your family stem from a refusal to observe the natural order God placed in your marriage?

Sister, in yielding to submission, you are not resigning yourself to doormat status. Remember, marriage is the image of the Trinity. Just as God the Father is head over His equal partners, Christ and the Holy Spirit, so is your husband head over you. He is your source, your leader. You are not inferior to him; you are valuable because you too carry the image of God. In the organization of marriage you just serve a different function than your husband. (We'll talk more about your vital role in chapter eight).

If up to this point in your marriage, you have gone along with your husband's ways with a reluctant heart, you have been an obedient wife but not a submissive wife. Obedience is what we expect from our children; it is not how you should respond to your husband. Submission flows from a willing heart, yielding your will even if you don't agree with or understand your husband's decisions. When you choose to defer to your husband's judgment and leadership, you present a picture of Christ to the world. Jesus always did things His Father's way, even if it was the difficult way. This is one way Jesus taught us to honor God.

One of the most important lessons I have learned about submission that has kept my heart focused and pure is to make Robert's decisions my decisions. When there is an issue to resolve in our family's life, Robert prays, asks me for counsel and then makes a decision. He does not always do what I think he should. But when he doesn't, I still walk beside him, in full support of his choice. Most of the time, things turn out great, and I stand beside him proudly. But in those times when he took us down the wrong path, I didn't blame him or play the victim. I stood beside him, encouraging him and facing the consequences with him.

Submission can be a scary decision, especially if your husband is not one who really seeks God's direction. Allow me to direct you to two more commands from God's Word: Above all else, submit to God (James 4:7), and only trust in Him (Proverbs 3:5). If your husband is not worthy of your submission, God will be there to take care of you. If I am submitting to the Lord by submitting to my husband, then I can confidently ask God to move on my behalf. When your husband's decision-making scares you, submit and pray. In Chapter 8, I will share more about how I've learned to make godly appeals when I am concerned about Robert's decisions. There is a way to approach your husband with your concerns in a submissive manner. Your first move though, should always be to plead your case to the Lord. And above all else, allow Him to work on your behalf.

Are you familiar with the book of Esther? It tells of two queens married to the same king at different times. Queen Vashti, the king's first wife, chose to dishonor her husband by refusing to submit to his wishes for her to attend his celebration. We are not told why she made such a foolish decision; perhaps the king deserved her contempt. Whatever her reasoning, she suffered the consequences of disrespecting her husband when he banished her from his presence forever.

Queen Esther took Vashti's place in the palace and undoubtedly learned from Vashti's mistake. When Esther uncovered a plot to destroy her people, the Jews, she was forced to consider what she must do to save them. Being queen, she might wield influence over the king; however, she knew she could not demand an audience with him and then order him around . . . her predecessor lived in exile for making that wrong move. Through fasting and prayer, Esther decided to honor the king with feasts and wait for the right time to ask for his favor. Her humble approach, respectful and reverent, pleased the king, and he granted her request. The entire Jewish nation was saved because of Esther's faith in God and respectful approach to her husband.

Esther can be a role model for us as wives, not only because she obeyed God by honoring her husband, but also because God used her for His high purposes because of her respectful spirit.

Should you feel like a Queen Vashti, locked out of your husband's thoughts, longing for the intimacy you once shared, I encourage you to change your approach to him. Start honoring him now, at every opportunity. Make a list of his great qualities. Rehearse all he is doing right, and then look for ways to brag on him. You will be amazed at how he will be drawn to you.

Treat your husband like royalty, the king of your home. He will be drawn to that throne of honor and will likely begin treating you more like the queen that you are as well.

CHAPTER 7

Sex: God's Gift to Marriage

Sitting across the table from a woman I will call Sharon, I tried not to look surprised as she disclosed her marriage life to me in hushed tones. Sharon, a bright, intelligent woman, had come to me after three years of marriage seeking relationship advice. Agreeing to meet her in a Dallas restaurant, I prayed and asked God to give me wisdom, not really expecting her problems to be different from those of other women I had counseled.

As she began sharing, I discovered that she and her husband Manuel were quite kind and cordial with one another. He was a great father, and they were not in financial debt. From what I could tell, they were managing married life beautifully. Knowing that she had approached me because they were having difficulties, I waited patiently for the conversation to center around the area of concern. I was not prepared for what Sharon revealed to me. She told me that there had been a lack of intimacy in their relationship for over two years.

Sharon and Manuel got pregnant as newlyweds. There were complications with the pregnancy, and the doctor recommended that they suspend sexual intercourse. After an arduous delivery, the young couple focused their attention and energy on caring for their newborn. Months went by and intimacy never returned. They managed to remain pleasant and considerate in their interactions, but never embraced, held hands, kissed or had sex. They had become roommates, splitting up the responsibilities of the home, sharing a bed but not giving themselves physically to each other.

The most shocking revelation in my conversation with Sharon came when she told me that neither she nor Manuel thought this lack of intimacy was strange. I was perplexed at their understanding of marriage and was confused about why Sharon had asked me to come to lunch. If they maintained a civil relationship and were both content with not having sex, I asked her what the problem in their marriage was. She told me that she feared Manuel might be interested in someone else.

Sharon's suspicions turned out to be accurate. Manuel had been involved with a woman from his office who had started working with him about six months prior to my lunch with Sharon. Though Manuel may have told his wife that he did not need sex to remain satisfied in his marriage, his actions betrayed his words. He ran to a woman who met his need for sexual intimacy because it was not being met at home.

Sexual intimacy plays a vital role in a healthy marriage. As women, we often minimize the importance of sex in our relationship with our husbands. Marriage expert Jimmy Evans, reporting on a survey, revealed a startling truth about men's and women's views on sex.[1] When asked to list their priorities, women placed sex at number thirteen, just after gardening. Men, on the other hand, ranked it at number two. Honor is their greatest need; sex is their second greatest need.

You are God's gift to your husband. He equipped you with everything you need to meet his needs. Just as you are to honor and respect him, you should also seek to meet his physical need for sex. As much as women complain about sex, I am always surprised to hear divorced and widowed women grieve over their loss of intimacy with their husbands. You have a need for affection, non-sexual and sexual, and you want your husband to meet that need. In fairness, let's try to understand our husbands' craving for sex.

Sex: God's Gift to Mankind

A talented auto mechanic had watched over and provided for his children for more than twenty years. No father could have loved his kids more; they were his delight and joy. When they were grown, they began to date and drift toward marriages of their own. This committed father wanted to give each one a special gift that they could cherish and enjoy when they started their own families. Since he was skilled with cars, he decided to build each one of them a specially crafted automobile that they could use and take pleasure in for years to come.

This father spent countless hours and invested thousands of dollars in each car, specially designing them to compliment each child. His oldest son was the first to marry. On his wedding day, the father revealed the car with a big red bow. His heart burst with pride and joy at the thought of his son driving down the road, his new wife nestled up next to him, with the top down and the wind blowing through their hair. What joy they would get from this gift!

Imagine the father's despair when he learned that his son had traded the car in for a work truck. "Dad," the son defended, "it's not that I didn't like the car. It's just that I needed something more practical for my job."

Heartbroken, the father turned to complete the car he had been working on for his daughter. On her wedding day, his hopes were high again as he presented his masterpiece to his precious baby girl. She and her husband could go on leisurely weekends together in their sporty coupe, and they'd be the envy of all their friends.

Sadly, again the father was devastated when he visited his daughter and son-in-law after six months and discovered that the car had never left the garage. "Dad," the young woman explained, "it is just too nice. The bus goes right by the house, so I just take it to work every day. Maybe when a special occasion comes around, then we'll use it."

Ladies, our heavenly Father created a special gift for each one of His married children as well. Many men trade their beautiful gift from God for what turns out to be an old work truck, and many women leave their beautiful gift from God in the garage and never enjoy it. While it is designed for practical purposes, it is also intended for pleasure. God wants us to delight in our spouse, enjoying sex as a lavish gift.

Does it surprise you that God wants you to enjoy sex? It may sound irreverent because many people see God as an old-fashioned, unemotional and distant deity who created man and woman but never intended for them to discover sex. Sweet sister, I pray that you will allow God to show you who He really is. Our Father is a passionate being. He created romance and intimacy and delights when we revel in them, because He too revels in them.

What would your sex life look like if you did it God's way? Do you think it would be exhilarating or boring? The sex-crazed culture we live in wants you to buy into the perverted distortion of a pleasurable sex life, but we could learn more if we went back to the Garden of Eden to see what it must have been like before sin distorted God's intent.

Before the fall of man, Adam and Eve lived naked and unashamed. Without selfishness to trip them up, they were completely sensitive and attentive toward each other. When they came together physically, it would have been a natural expression of their deep love. Neither would have used the other to meet their own needs. Their motivation was always to please the other person. Imagine how passionately and exhaustively they must have given themselves to one another. Sex was gratifying for both because each sought to meet the other's need.

Another place in Scripture we can look to discover God's heart for sex within marriage is the Song of Solomon. If you haven't ever read or studied this book, I highly encourage you to do so. It tells the story of a hot-blooded young couple in love and their experiences with romance and sex; yes, God put this book in the Bible! As the book opens, we read:

> *Let him kiss me with the kisses of his mouth —*
> *For your love is better than wine.*
> *Because of the fragrance of your good ointments,*
> *Your name is ointment poured forth;*
> *Therefore the virgins love you.*
> *Draw me away!*
>
> *(Song of Solomon 1:2-4)*

If you read the rest of the story, you will see how passionate God can be.

God made husbands and wives to be lovers. He wants you to be exhilarated with one another. While your husband may need sex more, it was created for you to enjoy as well. God gave you five senses with which to enjoy the world around you.

Consider how you take pleasure in God's creation: watching the sunrise, cuddling with a baby kitten, smelling the scent of the rain, listening to the crashing waves, and tasting freshly picked fruit. God fashioned us with the senses we needed to truly enjoy His creation. Friends, sex is another of God's gifts we were meant to fully experience and enjoy through our senses.

> *He brought me to the banqueting house,*
> *And his banner over me was love.*
> *Sustain me with cakes of raisins,*
> *Refresh me with apples,*
> *For I am lovesick.*
> *His left hand is under my head,*
> *And his right hand embraces me.*
>
> *(Song of Solomon 2:4-6)*

Do you see how both taste and touch are part of this young couple's passionate pursuit of intimacy? This is how God meant it to be. The Bible tells us, "Marriage is honorable among all, and the bed undefiled" (Hebrews 13:4). Sex is a holy act, and incorporating all of your senses into the marriage bed is what makes the experience healthy and satisfying. It may sound strange to say that sex is holy, but that is because our culture has robbed us of our innocence and has cheapened the gift that

God intended sex to be.

I remember when I first heard and understood this passage from Hebrews. Our pastor at the time, Olen Griffing, quoted it, and I was struck by its truth. For the first time in my life, I saw sex as a righteous act that God was pleased with. In a moment, lies that I had believed about sex were exposed, and I was free from their grip. I was released to explore this gift and to discover all it was meant to be.

Sexual intimacy is part of imaging God. As we come together selflessly, giving ourselves completely to serve our spouse, we look like Jesus as a selfless servant. As we come together passionately, we reflect our Father's picture of love given to us in the Song of Solomon. As we come together vulnerably, sharing intimacies that are ours alone, we demonstrate the Holy Spirit's willingness to reveal the Godhead to us unashamedly. Sex is beautiful and should be embraced by both husband and wife. When you give yourself to physical intimacy, you will be surprised what this shared closeness may give back.

Intimacy that Communicates

Your husband has a legitimate need for sex. You have a legitimate need for communication. Did you know that you can use one to accomplish the other? If you've tried everything you know how to talk some sense into your husband, consider what an active sex life would communicate to him.

First of all, when you place priority on your sex life, you are telling your husband that his needs are important to you. Does he know that his needs are important to you, or does he only know that your needs are important to you?

Another message that comes across loud and clear through a healthy sex life is acceptance. The vulnerable expression of sex shouts your approval of his manhood. When you refuse to have sex night after night, you are not just refusing sex, you are rejecting your husband. He does not feel wanted or loved by you when you continually turn him away.

Sex for your husband is an expression of his masculinity. Dr. Gary Rosberg explains that, "A man finds much of his own masculinity in his sexuality. This is part of our maleness; we can't erase it . . . no less than 50 percent and up to 90 percent of a man's self-image is locked up in his sexuality."[2] Your acceptance of him in bed tells him that you believe he is able to satisfy you and take care of you. Once he is convinced of your faith in him, he will be more likely to step up in places other than the bedroom. Your love acted out will give him the confidence he needs to be a godly husband and father as well as the courage he needs to live life as adventurously as God calls him to.

Jack Hayford explains in his book *Sex and the Single Soul:*[3]

I have found that wherever there is a breakdown in communication with a married couple, it virtually always traces back in some way to an absence of a mutually satisfying sexual relationship. The intimacy of a husband and wife's sexual relations – its act of complete self-disclosure, mutual surrender and unselfish giving – is the heart of the marriage relationship.

If communication is a problem between you and your husband, don't just look to him to talk to you more. Look to yourself to converse with him through sex.

A healthy sexual relationship is important to a healthy marriage relationship. There are dangers in ignoring the physical aspects of your marriage. Your husband will certainly feel rejected and he may even fall into the temptation of adultery in an attempt to have his need met. Maintaining a vivacious sex life keeps his eyes and heart turned toward you and fosters an atmosphere for healthy communication within the home.

Overcoming the Obstacles

Perhaps you have read this far and are cringing because no matter how important I tell you that sex is, you still don't want to make it a priority. Friend, your feelings are understandable. You are not alone in your discomfort or even distaste for physical intimacy. Satan has done an excellent job of building walls between women and their husbands for the purpose of obstructing sexual intimacy. The enemy knows how important sex is to a marriage and thus will stop at nothing to keep us from a healthy sex life.

Deception has always been Satan's greatest ally . . . this is where he got the name, "father of lies." Utilizing this crafty tool, he has convinced our culture of a mountain of lies about sex. Just to name a few: "Sex outside of marriage is fun and exciting." "You are only as valuable as you are sexy." "You aren't sexy if you don't have a supermodel body." "If you are a Christian, sex should be sterile and boring." Duped by the deception, many of us have come to believe that we should fulfill our marital obligation by just "grinning and bearing it."

Beloved, you have been lied to. Don't let this world or the devil tell you what sex should look like. Stop comparing yourself to magazine models and sitcom superstars. You were created perfectly imperfect – perfect because God's design is flawless and imperfect because you have a sin nature. We are all perfectly imperfect. You, however, are God's chosen one for your husband. Refuse to compare yourself to the unrealistic expectations of the world and instead strive to meet God's standard for a virtuous wife.

Satan also loves to lie to you about your husband. If you choose to listen to the fictitious tales the enemy spawns, you fall right into his hands and away from the embrace of your spouse. When he flaunts your husband's flaws and shortcomings before you, choose to forgive and give grace. Have you ever noticed that your husband looks less and less attractive the closer bedtime comes? This is Satan at work. He loves to start a fight right before you go to bed. If he can get you irritated at your husband, he knows there will be no intimacy, and his plot to destroy your marriage continues.

Satan uses lies to keep you away from sex because he knows that your mind is the most important sexual organ in your body. "The mind is the command center for all sexual feelings. It's the congress that governs your sexual state. It is the storehouse for every sexual thought you've ever had."[4] If Satan can distract your mind and prejudice your thoughts against your husband, he has succeeded in entrapping you in selfishness.

Just as darkness is expelled by light, deception is exposed by truth. There is no power in a lie when the truth is acknowledged. If you want to foil Satan's attacks on your marriage, you must start by fighting back on the battleground of your mind. You have to take every thought captive and determine whether it is true or false. Ask the Holy Spirit to show you truth about yourself, your husband and about sex. Evaluating ourselves in the light of truth is the only way out of the shadowy maze of deception and onto the straight path toward intimacy.

Most importantly you must be aware that deception is not Satan's only weapon, especially when you begin to catch him in his lies. He has a whole arsenal to choose from, and he will come at you from all directions once you decide to stand up to him.

One of the most common hindrances to a vibrant sex life in American homes is fatigue. In our always-on-the-go society, we have a hard enough time getting enough sleep. Who has time for sex? A recent poll revealed that 75 percent of people suffer from sleep problems such as insomnia, restlessness, snoring and fatigue. While experts recommend seven to nine hours of sleep a night for a healthy lifestyle, the average American gets only 6.9.[5]

Years ago, I was in one of those "super" seasons of life. Maybe you can relate. "S" was scripted on my well-worn super-hero outfit as I sought to be Super Mom, Super Wife, Super Employee, Super Friend and Super Pastor's Wife all at the same time. My typical day started at 5:30, and I went strong until about midnight, when I would collapse into bed, exhausted and completely spent.

One winter night, Robert approached me with romance in his eyes. "Let's sleep in front of the roaring fireplace tonight." When

I hesitated, he said, "Come on, let's do something spontaneous." Without thinking, I sighed and responded, "Let's do something spontaneous on Friday night instead."

We have laughed about this through the years, but I learned a powerful lesson that night. When I allow myself to live in a state of exhaustion, I miss golden opportunities for intimacy. If Satan can get me so busy taking care of everyone else, I won't have enough energy to take care of Robert. I wish I could say that I shredded my superhero costume that night, but unfortunately I didn't. Even today I have to reevaluate my priorities regularly to make sure that time for Robert keeps a top spot.

The last hindrance that I want to mention is the most difficult to bring up. Sometimes women have a hard time fully giving themselves physically to their husbands because of shame. For many of us, the road behind is a painful picture album of sin or abuse. Sex only opens the door to memories that we want to forget, memories of guilt and pain. How can we enjoy sex when every movement, every act, every sensation is tainted with shame?

Dear friend, God wants to set you free from that shame. Jesus died on the cross and bore all of our shame so that we wouldn't have to live under the weight of the past. Whether or not you were at fault for what happened, God wants you to experience full healing. Maybe you need forgiveness from God.

It is available to you freely. Maybe you need to forgive yourself. Maybe you need to forgive someone else. If you were abused, my heart goes out to you. Run to the arms of God and find comfort and peace. Wherever the fault lies, choose forgiveness and release yourself from the deadly grip of shame.

I have a friend whose stepfather sexually abused her for many years. Fortunately, she developed a deep love for the Lord by the time she was married. When she entered into that union with her husband, she went to God and asked Him to teach her what His desire for sex was. She had already experienced the dirty, abusive side of it, but she knew His heart intended so much more. Specifically, she asked God to heal her heart of the wounds of her past and then to teach her how to be a lover.

Over time, my friend received healing by forgiving both her stepfather and her mother. And through the years, she acquired another amazing testimony: "There were not many good Christian sources to teach me how to be a lover, but the Holy Spirit taught me." Even though her husband was not walking with the Lord, they established godly boundaries and explored within those boundaries. Years later, when her husband came to know the Lord, nothing changed in their love life because he was happy with the blessed sex life God already had given them.

God is using my friend's life as a testimony to other Christian women. A few years ago at a women's retreat, one lady was commenting on her disgust with sex. My friend replied, "What's not to like?" This opened up a very honest discussion among the whole group and set the stage for my friend to share her story. God had granted her a healthy respect for the beauty of sex despite her introduction to its destructive side as a child.

God wants you to move beyond the abuse and shame that have plagued you for years. He wants to heal the deep recesses of your heart so that you can enjoy His gift of sex within marriage. I am not an expert in healing brokenness, but God is. Run to Him!

Friends, sex will never reach its full potential in your marriage as long as there are selfish motives. In 1 Corinthians 7:3-5 we read,

> *Let the husband render to his wife the affection due her, and likewise also the wife to her husband. The wife does not have authority over her own body, but the husband does. And likewise the husband does not have authority over his own body, but the wife does. Do not deprive one another except with consent for a time, that you may give yourselves to fasting and prayer; and come together again so that Satan does not tempt you because of your lack of self-control.*

Paul exhorts us here to die to our own flesh and come alive for the purpose of fulfilling our spouse's desires. Sex can be heaven on earth for you and your husband when both of you give yourselves to it the way God intended.

Make a Change Today

If you have a vibrant sex life already, protect and cherish it. Nourish it so that Satan does not steal the intimacy you already are blessed with. If your relationship looks more like Sharon and Manuel's, make a commitment to start improving it today.

The best way to start developing a healthy sex life is to pray. If praying about sex sounds strange, remember that God created sex. In His eyes it is a beautiful gift meant for you to enjoy with your husband. If we assume God will be displeased with us coming to Him to ask about sex, we will likely go somewhere else for information and encouragement. We already have discovered that the world and Satan are waiting to feed us lies. Trust the Holy Spirit to teach you about sex.

One great tool God has given us to learn about sex is the Song of Solomon. Read it, either alone or with your spouse. As you read, ask the Holy Spirit to give you His heart for sex. Over time, you will notice a difference in your approach to and enjoyment of sexual intimacy.

Finally, remember that not all marital struggles are rooted

in the bedroom. Other issues such as financial trouble, sick children or work problems might be weighing heavily on your relationship. Deal with such matters openly. Talk about them so that the stress doesn't pour over into the bedroom.

Sharon and Manuel never reconciled. By the time she sought help, he was already emotionally and sexually entrenched in another relationship. While adultery is never excusable, I wonder, if she had reached out to him earlier, would the outcome have been different? In my heart I believe that if a vibrant sexual relationship had been in place, the door of opportunity for the other woman to step through would never have been opened.

Sex was God's creation, not man's. It was created for pleasure by a loving Father who desires that His children experience true intimacy. In the beauty of marriage, we should allow ourselves to live in the richest of God's blessings. Enjoy God's gift to you. Experience a piece of Eden by giving yourself completely to pursue love in its most passionate form.

CHAPTER 8

Breaking into the
He-Man Woman Hater's Club

The 1994 movie *The Little Rascals* reintroduced us to characters from the classic series: Spanky, Buckwheat, Alfalfa and Darla. The Little Rascals were a group of boys who joined together to form the He-Man Woman Hater's Club. Their unifying vow was to hate girls. Alfalfa constantly battled allegiance, because, while he wanted to be a part of the gang, his heart belonged to a charming little brunette, Darla.

Stymie, a young member in good standing with the He-Man Woman Hater's Club, recited the club pledge with conviction: "I, Stymie, do solemnly swear to be a he-man and hate women and not play with them or talk to them unless I have to, and especially never fall in love; and if I do, may I die slowly and painfully and suffer for hours – or until I scream bloody murder."

Perhaps your husband joined the He-Man Woman Hater's Club as a little boy and has never fully revoked his membership. Obviously, he broke the vow about never falling in love, but he still clings to some of the old ways, roping off portions of his heart and life with a bright yellow tape that reads: "Keep Out! Property of the He-Man Woman Hater's Club."

As women, we are designed to connect and communicate on intimate, emotional levels. Our husbands, on the other hand, are not wired like we are. In his message to the men earlier in this book, Robert explained that one reason God gave woman to man was to help him connect emotionally. Females bear God's emotional image. We are passionate, empathetic, intuitive and sensitive, just like God is. Men can never know and understand God fully unless they learn to connect on an emotional level.

Ladies, you need to go deep with your husband, and he needs you to teach him how to go deep with you. Your desire to break into his little club is not an ungodly desire. God wants you to connect to your husband for two reasons: To increase intimacy in your marriage and to help him connect more deeply with his heavenly Father. Your desire to open your husband's heart is from God, but your methods in doing so might not be pleasing to Him.

How should we go about getting into those hearts? Men can be very protective of their restricted areas. Their memories and feelings are housed in a clubhouse of sorts, divided and compartmentalized with various access levels requiring visitors to earn security clearance before entrance is granted. Even if your husband pretends to be an emotional rock, the reality is that his feelings are very sensitive, and he goes to extreme measures to protect his heart.

When you were dating, your husband granted you limited access to his clubhouse. As he determined what you needed to know, he unlocked different rooms and let you in. Maybe he first ushered you into his trophy room in attempts to impress you with his accomplishments. Some men rush women through the house straight to the bedroom and try to keep them locked up there. More than likely, he spent a lot of time with you in the game room . . . that tends to be one of the favorite places to hang out. When he first met your father, maybe he unlocked the office to prove his financial stability. For your pastor, maybe he opened up the study and amazed you both with his knowledge.

With each open door, you got to know your husband a little bit better. Because you are a woman, you probably fell in love with him when he gave you glimpses into those dark rooms that housed his deepest memories and most cherished dreams. By allowing you into his heart, he communicated to you that he wanted to be intimate with you. Women can seldom turn away from such vulnerability.

Now, though, you are married . . . and he has clammed up. It's almost like he opened up those places in his heart just to win you over and now that he has you, he has bolted the door shut denying you any further access. Dear sister, in order to achieve the intimacy the Father wants you to have in marriage, you have to get into those rooms. Attempting to beat down the door or sneak in through a window will only result in tighter security measures. Instead, you should learn to follow entry procedures that grant the access you need.

Gaining Entrance to His Heart

I want to know Robert Morris inside and out. I want a level of intimacy that goes beyond sex, beyond the common bond of family and raising children together. I want to know what he thinks, why he thinks it and how he feels. True intimacy requires vulnerability and transparency; guarded hearts are protected by walls that restrict closeness. Men, regardless of their rough exteriors, are as fragile emotionally as women are physically. Only if you try to understand him and treat his emotional side with care will you be allowed into his secret place. After almost twenty-six years of marriage, I have found great joy in knowing Robert through complete transparency and tender vulnerability. I've seen into his heart, where he stores his hopes and dreams, fears and failures, prayers and memories. Robert and I have shared the deepest parts of our souls with one another. He has no secrets from me, and I have none from him.

This openness did not spring up over night; it was cultivated over time. I had to learn how to approach the quarantined areas of his past, and in doing so I've learned some valuable lessons that I would like to pass on to you.

Enter Quietly

First, if you expect your husband to give you unrestricted access to his heart, you must be willing to enter with etiquette. If your friend invited you to her home, would you walk in and start rearranging, redecorating or insulting her belongings? No, you would respect her space and choices. Why then do we tend to walk into our husbands lives and pasts with an air of disapproval?

When your husband invites you into his trophy room and you see a picture of his first girlfriend hanging on the wall, don't react out of personal insecurity by remarking that she was fat or ugly. While he might agree with you or act unhurt, he will not likely tell you about old girlfriends any more. When you respond to his vulnerability with judgment or cruelty, he recoils and pushes you back out the door. You can't enter his heart with the goal of setting up your throne and taking over. His past and feelings are already there, and you must be willing to accept them no matter what.

In contrast, every time you welcome your husband's past with open arms, you earn his confidence. When he knows he can trust you with small parts of his heart, he will begin to trust you with more. You vowed to love your husband when you married him, and accepting his past no matter what it looks like reminds him that your love for him is unconditional and lasting.

Redecorating is Not Allowed

The second rule of entry is: Reorganizing and redecorating are not allowed. You may be able to accept your husband's past, but you might find it more difficult to accept who he is today without trying to change him. Only God can change hearts and minds . . . you can't. When you discover something in your husband's heart that is less than virtuous, give it to the Lord. Your goal in going deep is becoming one with the husband you have, not trying to create a new husband altogether.

When I hear of couples who divorce after twenty-plus years of marriage, I wonder when they lost intimacy. They locked each other out, concealing secret dreams and hopes, and eventually they felt like they were sleeping with a stranger. If we don't stay connected at the soul level, we slowly drift apart until it appears we share nothing except a mortgage. Enter your husband's heart cherishing the intimacy you find there; don't force him to change.

No Demands

Third, don't demand entry. Tell me that I can't, and I will go out of my way to prove you wrong. So many times, when we as women encounter that yellow restricting tape, we scheme and plot to find another way in. We try to manipulate with guilt saying, "I am your wife. I can't believe you won't tell me about that." Tears never help our cause either. Though manipulation temporarily gets us what we want, it always mutates and becomes our greatest enemy. Your husband will start to recognize your manipulative games and will resent you for them. He will shut you out, and however much the door was opened to you before, it will be slammed back in your face. His heart will grow hard toward you, and intimacy will slip from your grip. So, instead of forcing your way in, wait on him to open the door. He will in his own time; just be patient.

If you approach your husband with acceptance, appreciation and patience, your venture into his heart will be a successful one, rewarded with a newfound closeness. But how do you actually get into his heart? Some of those doors are barred and padlocked, and the hinges are even rusted over because it has been so long since the door was opened! Allow me to share some practical steps you can take to gain entry.

Above all, you have to approach the door with humility. Barging in won't work. Banging and yelling won't do the trick. More than likely, an abrasive approach will remind him of his sixth grade English teacher who was always on his case or his mother who constantly badgered him. Years of annoyance have taught him to ignore such harsh tactics.

You must be different; you must knock gently. You may be surprised at how far a simple knock will get you.

Once you knock, understand that he decides whether or not to answer. This goes back to the not forcing entry rule. One trick to increasing your chances of getting in is to consider the timing of your knock. You can humbly knock as soon as he walks in the door after a congested commute and a long exhausting day at work . . . and you can guarantee being denied. You can gently knock when he is in the middle of paying bills . . . and again you will find rejection. Men are more prone to communicate in a relaxed setting. When you want him to be vulnerable with you, create a comfortable atmosphere and allow him to loosen up before you start knocking.

Now, what do I mean when I tell you to "knock"? Knocking is as simple as asking a question. God has used this method of knocking on man's heart since the beginning of time. When Adam and Eve first sinned, he came to them and asked, "Where are you?" (Genesis 3:9). God probed into Abraham's heart of faith by asking, "Is anything too hard for the Lord?" (Genesis 18:14). Drawing Saul to repentance on the road to Damascus, Jesus asked, "Saul, Saul, why are you persecuting Me?" (Acts 9:4).

Questions turn the key that unlocks the heart. They

probe into our subconscious, forcing us to confront our perceptions and pasts. When asked in humility at opportune moments, they uncover your husband's heart with honesty and sincerity. His answers to your questions take you on the tour of his heart that you have longed for. Your loving reception of his revelation is the acceptance he feared he would never find. You knock. He lets you in. You ask. He answers. Intimacy is deepened.

When my friend Kimberly was worried about a business decision that her husband was making, she grew frustrated because he turned a deaf ear to her concerns. I suggested that she pose questions to her husband instead of voicing apprehensions. She began asking things like, "What are you going to do if this happens?" and "How will you feel if this doesn't go through as you hope?" Her new approach gave her the opportunity to hear his point of view and understand him better. He in turn was more open to exploring her perspective. The tension began to lessen because they were communicating their motives, fears and hopes.

Ladies, your husband is far more likely to change his mind in response to a question that causes him to rethink his position than if you blast him with your opinion. Men are created with an ego that, apart from Christ, makes it difficult to admit even the possibility that they may be wrong.

In chapter six, we talked about submission. One of the scariest risks of submission is that you give your husband carte blanche to make bad decisions for your family. As a godly companion for your husband, you need to know how to communicate and express your concern in a manner that does not contradict your submission.

Think back through the story of Esther. She had to confront her husband, the king, about one of his trusted leaders who was plotting the annihilation of her people, the Jews. How she made her appeal could mean the deliverance of her people or the destruction of every man, woman and child.

The first thing Esther did was prepare herself. She fasted and enlisted others to fast and pray with her (Esther 4:16). Surely during this season of prayer, she asked God what she should say and how she should say it. Once she knew she had God's covering and favor, she positioned herself before the king so that she could speak to him. Dressed in her royal robes, she went to the inner courts to be noticed by him. While it didn't hurt her situation to be dressed attractively, it was even more important that she dress in humility through prayer and fasting. Remember, approaching your husband with humility could be the difference between him listening to you or tuning you out.

Esther waited for the right time to present her appeal to

the king. She had several opportunities, some where he even offered her up to half of the kingdom! Scripture does not tell us why Esther passed up these opportunities, but it is obvious that God was working through the timing (Esther 5). When God prompted her at the right moment, she petitioned the king with meekness and confidence (Esther 7:3-4). She had complete faith in God to take care of the outcome because she had been obedient. God honored her faith and boldness by giving her favor in the eyes of her husband. The whole Jewish nation was saved, and the king's corrupt advisor was killed instead.

Submitting to your husband's headship does not mean surrendering your voice in his life. When you make an appeal to his judgment and decisions, apply the same rules I gave you earlier in knocking on your husband's heart: Commit ahead of time to accept his response no matter what it is; trust God to change his heart and refuse to force your side on him; approach him with humility at the right time.

The Intimacy He Craves

I know that the desire of your heart is to be close to your husband. We both know that this is God's desire for your marriage as well. You feel close to him when he opens up to you, sharing the deepest parts of his soul. Intimacy is fostered during these times, but there are other ways to cultivate intimacy as well.

Your husband will never trust you enough to open up if he does not feel comfortable with you. One of his greatest needs is for companionship. Yes, he needs respect and sex, but he also needs someone to spend his life with. Adam was lonely because he had no one like him to share his life with. God, in His all-knowing generosity, gave Adam a wife.

Men and women are very different. As women grow older, we generally lose the taste for childhood games and sports. Fun for us is shopping and dinner parties. Men, on the other hand, never outgrow good old-fashioned fun. They love to play! You know I am right. Their need for companionship is closely tied to their love of play time. Your husband wants to share fun times with you.

Before they married, Shelly was always a good sport about trying all of Bill's recreational activities. As newlyweds, they went hunting, fishing and camping together all the time. After a couple years of marriage and with the arrival of their first child, Shelly lost interest in going on these "smelly" trips. With her blessing, Bill went with friends, leaving her behind to go to the movies or shopping with her friends. At the time, neither thought these separate recreational lives were dangerous to their relationship.

Years later, after their children were grown and out of the house, Shelly and Bill had to face a harsh reality: They were lost in each other's presence. While they shared a house, a family and even a past, they did not know what to do with the moments they were forced to share each day in an empty nest. Because they had not nurtured their relationship over all of those years, they had no companionship to enjoy in their retirement.

This story is common. While dating, young people are willing to do anything to spend time with one another. A young man will walk all over the mall carrying packages just to be with his girlfriend. A young woman will sleep on the ground, miles from civilization, putting worms on a fishing hook just to spend time with her boyfriend. After the wedding, though, those activities lose their appeal. What couples don't realize is that, just as new love is nurtured by spending time in some form of recreation, old love matures with time shared together! The cares of work and family can make the fun side of your emotions seem unimportant, but building companionship through mutually enjoyable activities is imperative.

I have at least attempted all of Robert's favorite pastimes. There are a few that Robert and I agree I am not suited for. A scuba excursion that ended in a near-death experience showed us that diving may not be an activity we can enjoy together. An embarrassing incident involving our golf cart and tire tracks across the green taught us that golf might not be the best team sport for our marriage either. But when Robert gets tickets to a hockey game, the first person he calls to join him is me. I still go camping and fishing with him and have learned to really enjoy those excursions. Robert loves to have fun with me, and I love being the one he has fun with. We are best friends, and I know that being his best friend makes it easier for him to open up to me when there is something on his heart and mind.

Giver of Life

Do you know what the name "Eve" means? It means "living; enlivening"[1] or "life giver."[2] Adam received Eve as a gift, and her influence on his world caused him to call her "the one who has made my world come alive." Dear friend, you can do the same for your husband. As the woman God has given to your husband, you stand poised to open the world of emotions to him. Your enthusiasm and unique giftedness can brighten and improve his world. Even more, just as Eve conceived and gave birth to the first baby, so you have the ability to conceive and give birth to your husband's dreams.

Sixteen years ago, I delivered our last child. However,

my work as a life-giver was not over. Since that time, I have born dreams with Robert and seen them come to full fruition. In 2000, Robert had a dream to start a church. We had never started a church before, so we were uncertain of all that it would require. A flood of questions nagged at us, and scenarios of failure harassed our faith. Personally, I wondered what would happen if it didn't work out. Would we be able to send our high school age boys to college? How would our friendships hold up if we moved away?

I had dozens of opportunities to discourage Robert's dream. In so many ways, it seemed impractical and risky. However, I knew that God was calling us to believe Him. For me, faith meant turning a deaf ear to doubts and questions so that I could stand confidently by my husband. Faith loves friends who stand alongside to believe. As a faith-filled companion, you can spur your husband's faith to new levels. As a doubting companion, you will destructively tear down his faith. We must be life-giving wives to our husband's dreams if we want to see them reach their full potential.

Creating an encouraging haven for your husband's dreams motivates him to confide in you. His heart is much more likely to open if he knows he will find a friend that will give his dreams wings to fly.

Life Comes from the Spirit

God ordained you to be the life-giver in your marriage. The part you play is vital if you and your husband ever hope to experience the blessing of God's ultimate potential being reached in your family. But you cannot be a life-giver day after day if you are not drawing life at the same time. John tells us that, "It is the Spirit who gives life; the flesh profits nothing" (John 6:63). You cannot be a godly wife in your own strength, because your flesh profits nothing. However, if you enter into a partnership with God, He will continuously give you life through His Spirit so that you can pass that life onto your husband and children.

Jesus promised you that, "If you abide in Me, and My words abide in you, you will ask what you desire, and it shall be done for you. By this My Father is glorified, that you bear much fruit; so you will be My disciples" (John 15:7-8). Abiding in Christ is the key to bearing fruit, giving life. To abide in Him, you must spend time with God. Making your relationship with the Lord priority is the only way you can be sure to stay connected to the ultimate life-giver. Take time every day, asking God to fill you with His life. Allow His Spirit to impress on your heart Scriptures to read, thoughts to meditate on and commands to obey.

Allow God to enliven your world as you make your relationship with Him the first priority in your life. Trust Him to take care of you and use you for His Kingdom purposes. When you walk closely with God, your relationship with your husband becomes easier. Filled with the Spirit of God, you will be able to honor your spouse with your words and actions. Submission will come more naturally as you are made more into the image of Christ. Life will flow through you to your husband's hopes and dreams. As you draw closer to the heart of God, your husband will learn from you how to connect to the Father more intimately. Your unwavering commitment and service to him will meet the needs in his life so that he will not be tempted to look outside your relationship for satisfaction.

My dear friends, a blessed marriage waits for you. God does not hold it back from us; He extends His blessing openhandedly, waiting for us to receive it as a gift. Your destiny lies in denying your fleshly desires so that you can be the companion your husband needs. When you meet his needs, you are fulfilling your calling in life.

You hold life for your husband. Don't keep it from him; pour it out, overflowing, abundant and transforming.

CHAPTER 9

Forgiving through
the Hard Times

"Over your dead body," thought Terri. Once again, her husband, Frank, had gone too far. He'd hurt her and wanted forgiveness. Well, with this transgression added to the long list that had been building for years, how could he ever expect her to forgive him?

To the outside world, Frank and Terri's marriage seemed healthy and successful. They'd been together for more than ten years and were very involved in their church. They tithed faithfully and sought to train their three sons with biblical truth. But while they appeared solid to the outside world, their home life was teetering on the brink of devastation. Besides the growing tension between husband and wife, two of their sons faced major medical problems. One suffered from a rare illness and needed surgery that would leave him in a body cast for weeks. The other fought asthma that was becoming more and more difficult to manage.

One day, seemingly out of the blue, Frank approached Terri with the news that he was planning to divorce her. Totally shocked, she thought, *"I should be the one leaving you; I am the innocent one in this marriage."*

Terri and Frank's story is a common one. The hallmark of relationship is conflict. This is especially true for a married couple. Living together, sharing everything from drawer space to children, you are bound to get in each other's way and step on each other's toes. He leaves his dirty socks on the floor, and she forgets to write the check amount in the ledger. He complains about dinner while ruling the remote control, and she paints her toenails while talking on the phone during the big game. As long as married couples live together, we will irritate one another. The question is, how are you going to let tensions affect your marriage?

Ruth Bell Graham has been married to the internationally-known evangelist Billy Graham for more than sixty years. She and Billy both have tremendous reputations for godliness. When asked about their successfully long marriage, Ruth testified that, "marriage is the union of two good forgivers."

Unless you are living in total denial, your spouse did something today that totally annoyed you (be honest). And what's worse, beyond the common frustrations of forgetting to take out the trash or throwing out your favorite old T-shirt, he or she has said or done things that have hurt you deeply. You've been violated, mistreated, forgotten and unappreciated. Over and over, your love is tested when your spouse falls short of the high standard of love. That is why forgiveness is absolutely necessary if you want your marriage to last.

Without conflict, marriage would be easy and your love would never be tested. How could your husband or wife ever experience the unconditional love of Christ through you if they never needed grace or forgiveness? Does anyone ever really deserve to be forgiven? Do you? Just as Jesus sacrificed Himself so that we could be restored to a right relationship with God, so you must learn to sacrifice and forgive so that your marriage can thrive in reconciliation.

Exposing the Enemy's Arsenal

Above all, Satan is a liar (John 8:44). He is the great deceiver, bent on entrapping us in the dark cloud that deception creates. Paul told us that Satan is also the "prince of the power of the air" (Ephesians 2:2). In Revelation 12:10, Satan is called the "accuser of our brethren." By putting these three descriptions together, we begin to see how he works against us to tear down our marriages. You may not realize it but Satan manipulates your words and thoughts, mutating them into insults and allegations against your spouse.

Husbands, a minor example might be when you come home and ask your wife, "When is dinner going to be ready?" Those words must travel through the air before they land in the ear and communicate to your wife. Who lurks in the air, waiting to weave falsehood from reality? Satan. He loves to take your words and twist them around before they land on your wife's eardrums. By the time your question arrives, she hears,

"Isn't dinner ready yet?" Wives, an example for you is when your gentle reminder that, "Trash pick up is in the morning," ends up being heard, "Get up, you lazy bum, and take out the trash!" Satan, the liar, uses his power and dominion in the air to fabricate insults from your spouse that will trigger a defensive remark from you thus starting a fight. Satan has perfected his manipulation to such an art that we seldom question whether we have misheard or misunderstood others.

Once the twisted truth enters your ear, Satan goes to work accusing your spouse even further. He reminds you of all the things he or she has done wrong in the past. He suggests possible meanings behind the words that are hurtful or irritating. He incites fear and insecurity by causing you to doubt truth. He is a liar, a manipulator and an accuser, yet too often we allow him to reign in our marriages.

After the offense has occurred, Satan doesn't leave it to rest in your mind. Instead, he picks at your wounds until they fester, infecting your whole outlook toward your husband or wife. He convinces you that you should not forgive because he or she doesn't deserve it. Somehow you believe that your bitterness causes the other pain.

Choosing not to forgive is like drinking poison and hoping the other person gets sick from it. While we wait and watch for any indication of remorse, the poison eats away at our own souls and eventually kills us. Like Terri, we sip the poison when we allow small or large offenses to go without forgiveness. With every sin, we have the opportunity to forgive or not, a choice to swallow life or death.

Have you truly forgiven your husband or wife for the countless disappointments and wounds? A good litmus test to determine the sincerity of your forgiveness is to think about his or her indiscretion for a few minutes and see if your musing turns to annoyance or anger. Another good indicator that you have not forgiven is if the act consumes your mind and conversation. When you truly forgive, anger leaves along with the need to vent.

Unforgiveness is also apparent when you refuse to let go of the offense. While it may be humanly impossible to forget what happened, we have a choice whether to dwell on it or use it as manipulative leverage in the future. There will be situations when the past must be discussed in order to achieve reconciliation and healing, but this should be the only reason we bring up what has already been forgiven. Mentioning it for any other reason will only result in heaping shame and guilt on your spouse. Peace cannot coexist with disgrace and blame.

Jesus gave us a great illustration of the importance of forgiveness in a story he told about a king and a servant (Matthew 18:23-35). The king had been generous in making loans to his subjects but one day decided to settle all of the accounts. This was bad news for one particular servant who owed far more than he could pay. In order to reconcile the debt, the king ordered that the servant and his whole family be sold into slavery until the money was paid. Afraid for his family and future, the servant fell on his face and begged for more time to pay the debt. Moved to compassion, the king had mercy on the servant, releasing him and not requiring him to pay any portion of the balance.

Certainly relieved, the servant left the king's presence. He then sought out another servant who owed him an amount far less than he had owed the king. Violently, he demanded the money from his fellow servant. In similar fashion to the first servant's plea to the king, the second servant begged for more time to make amends. Without mercy, the first servant had his associate thrown in prison until the debt was paid.

Word got back to the king about the man's ghastly treatment of another indebted subject. Infuriated, he called the servant to his presence and corrected him:

> "I forgave you all that debt because you begged me. Should you not also have had compassion on your fellow servant, just as I had pity on you?"
>
> (Matthew 18:32-33)

He then delivered the servant to the torturers until he could pay the original debt.

Friends, Jesus made the ultimate sacrifice to pay a debt we could never have worked off in all of eternity. Our forgiveness came at a steep price, but Jesus paid it, and we have received the blessings of a gracious king. Now, what is our response to those who wrong us? Do they deserve our forgiveness? Did we deserve God's forgiveness?

We have a choice. Every time our spouse messes up, whether insignificantly or royally, we have the opportunity to extend the same mercy and forgiveness we received from Christ. We can pass on the grace that was bestowed on us, or we can insist on punishing by refusing to forgive. What we learn from the parable is that, in our attempts to penalize others, we really sentence ourselves to torture. God intended for us to receive forgiveness and move forward in the freedom it provides. Unforgiveness robs us of that chance, holding us captive to our past state of bankruptcy.

Satan, as we have already discussed, sits poised to destroy your marriage. He will lie, manipulate and accuse to get his way. Since he was kicked out of heaven, he has worked to bring the world down with him. We are not going to change his ways, but sometimes without realizing, we supply the weapons the enemy needs to strategically attack our spouses.

When you determine that there are certain offenses your spouse can commit that are unforgivable, you give Satan a list of ways to tempt and trap him or her that will result in a defeated marriage. Perhaps you have been generous in forgiving your husband for forgetting your birthday and being lazy around the house. Maybe you have gone out of your way to pardon your wife's mood swings and big mouth. But men, what if she racked up some huge credit card bills that forced you to work overtime to pay off? Ladies, what if you discovered that your husband has frequented pornographic websites for years? What if you found out about an affair?

The devil is crafty, and he will push you to your limit. The world will tell you that everyone has a breaking point, and you are not expected to put up with too much. If you give in to this attitude, Satan will have an easy time pushing you over the edge of unforgiveness.

Positioned to Forgive

Forgiveness is a rewarding virtue. Jesus told us that as we forgive others, we are forgiven by God (Matthew 6:14). Forgiving others kills the bitterness that eats at our hearts and restores a healthy relationship. It also frees your life from sin so that you can be a conduit of further blessing for your family. But forgiveness does not just pop into your heart, like joy or fear. It is not a natural response to pain. It is a choice.

What do you think would happen if you determined ahead of time that there is nothing your husband or wife could do that you would not forgive? Your spouse would still make mistakes, maybe even big mistakes, but when these times came up, your marriage would not be in danger of termination because you had already decided to forgive.

Remember, our marriages image God. We show the world what He is like by how we interact with one another. Psalm 86:5 says (empahsis added):

> *For You, Lord, are good, and* ready to forgive,
> *And abundant in mercy to all those who call upon You.*

Our heavenly Father is ready, poised to forgive us no matter what we do. There is nothing you or I could do that would cause Him to divorce us! His forgiveness is not limited but boundless. We must imitate His resolve in our marriages so that others can see how gracious and merciful He is.

Can you do it? Today, can you look at your spouse and declare aloud for all to hear (including Satan), "No matter what you do, I will choose to forgive you"? Speaking these words with sincerity will be a turning point in your marriage, calming your lover with assurance and disarming Satan of his schemes.

Is this too hard to do right now? Your inability to forgive ahead of time is understandable because your pain from past grievances is real. We can't expect it to be dissolved in a moment. Several years ago, Robert and I were wronged by an individual, and I had a very difficult time forgiving. I would rerun his hurtful actions over and over in my mind and then practice conversations where I would put him in his place. I so desperately wanted to have the final word with a kick in the chin as the exclamation point. Months went by, and still I was unable to forgive this man.

Then, I heard a pastor preach on forgiveness. He suggested that we pray for whomever we were having trouble forgiving and bless them. Well, there was no desire in my heart to pray for this person, much less bless him, but I knew I was trapped by my unforgiveness and that I needed to do something. So, every time I caught myself thinking about the situation, I turned my thoughts into a prayer. At first, my teeth clinched as I uttered words of blessing, but over time I was surprised to discover that my feelings toward him were changing. Soon, the bitterness was gone, and my mind was free from the exhausting wear of unforgiveness.

Perhaps your spouse has hurt you so many times that you find it difficult to say, "I have decided to forgive you even when you hurt me in the future." Start by praying. Ask God to shower blessings on his life; pray for healing and change in her life. While you are at it, ask God to change your heart so that you will be able to forgive. If you expect to survive the sudden blows of marriage, you must posture yourself to forgive. The only position you can consistently offer forgiveness from is one where you can clearly see yourself and your spouse in light of God's infinite grace and mercy.

God changes you through prayer. It is through consistent conversation that you gain the mind of Christ. I (Robert) have also struggled with forgiveness. I remember once talking to God about a friend who had really done me wrong. God was telling me to forgive him, and I was fighting Him. "Lord, he was wrong!" I protested.

The Lord's reply to me was pointed, cutting to my heart, "Yes, Robert, he was wrong . . . that is why you need to forgive him. If he were right, he wouldn't need your forgiveness!" Sometimes God's view of a situation can be annoyingly accurate. His words gave me the mind of Christ, teaching me the grace I needed to forgive the offense. Be honest with God about your feelings, and then trust Him to change you.

Power of Forgiveness

Nabel was a successful businessman in Israel during David's lifetime. Nabel's shepherds had encountered David in the wilderness, and David had treated them with kindness and protection. When the religious feast season came about, David sent word to Nabel, blessing him and asking if he and his companions could join him for the feast. Instead of returning David's kindness, Nabel scorned him and refused to extend a hand of hospitality. Upon receiving Nabel's message, David assembled a small army and set out to attack his household.

Abigail, Nabel's beautiful and wise wife, heard what had happened between her husband and David. Quickly, she gathered a generous gift and set out to make peace with David before her family was killed. She approached David humbly and pleaded for mercy. He was moved by her appeal and relented from his assault (1 Samuel 25:1-35).

As Nabel's wife, Abigail held great influence in her arbitration with David. In the same way, when we choose to forgive our spouses and pray on their behalf, mercy and blessing are poured out because of our requests. Knowing this, we should not only determine to forgive, we should also resolve to intercede boldly. We can and should pray that the sins we make as parents will not be passed down to our children. We can and should pray for wisdom with our finances, so that our poor past management can guide us to solid biblical principles. We can and should pray for healing and restoration when adultery has ripped a hole in our hearts. We must be bold, not settling for a mere mending, but insisting on a greater restoration of passionate fellowship and newfound unity. You made a covenant before God on your wedding day, and God looks at you not just as an individual but as one with your partner. Your position within the marriage gives you authority in prayer over your spouse that has potential for life-changing and life-enhancing blessing.

In the early years of our marriage, Robert made a really bad decision that caused us grief for many years. Because I was not included in the decision, I played the victim and wallowed in my pain. When I would pray, I would say things like, "Lord, smite your foolish and stubborn servant Robert Morris!" (I used words like "smite" because I thought it sounded more spiritual.) I would have been satisfied if fire had fallen down from heaven on him.

One day I realized though, that by praying down punishment on Robert, I was putting myself in danger. You see, I am one with Robert and thus the fires of vengeance aimed at him would likely burn me as well. Quickly, I repented of my anger and unforgiveness and instead began interceding on Robert's behalf. As I asked for mercy and wisdom for him, God began to show me the power I had in prayer over my husband because I am one with him. God responds to my prayers for him more than any other because we are one. He has proven this to me over and over because when I pray on Robert's behalf, God moves.

Advice for the Offender

There are two sides to every conflict. So far, we have devoted this whole chapter to the offended. The one who receives the blow needs to forgive, but we don't want to ignore the one who throws the punch. Seldom in an argument is one person completely right. Most often both sides are guilty of something. Sometimes, when we are praying to receive the mind of Christ so that we can forgive, the Holy Spirit shows us that we are not the only victims. Each of us has to admit, as much as others have hurt us, we have wronged them as well.

If you are the offender, ask God to show you the severity of your offense. Debbie and I were counseling with a couple one time where the man had inappropriately engaged in sexual discussions with a woman from his office. His wife was obviously very hurt, and her eyes were swollen and red from crying.

The man openly shared about how God was working in his life through the situation. As he was talking, God opened my eyes to see the severity of the situation. Before I could stop myself, I blurted out, "You make me sick!" Stunned, the man stopped talking and stared wide-eyed at me. Debbie and the wife also looked at me in disbelief, wondering what had come over me.

God had shown me the tremendous hurt and betrayal that young wife was experiencing. I continued, "You make me sick! Your wife is sitting over there, bawling her eyes out, and you are telling me how much God is working in your life. You are completely insensitive to the pain she is feeling right now! You haven't beaten her physically, but you have beaten her emotionally and broken her heart. It's like she is sitting there with two black eyes, a bloody lip and a broken nose while you go on and on about how much God has used this situation in your life. You should be on your knees in front of her, begging her forgiveness and committing the rest of your life to honor and serve her!"

Sometimes when we offend, we don't realize how much we have hurt the other person and therefore our repentance does not match our crime. Until we are able to repent to the same degree that we offended, there will not be the emotional restoration that is needed to heal the relationship. Ask God to show you the blackened eyes of your spouse's soul so that you can repent appropriately.

Hopefully, if your husband or wife has been reading this book with you, he or she will be positioned to forgive you when you mess up. But whether forgiveness is waiting, it is your responsibility to confess and repent. Repentance involves changing your mind and changing your direction. It is not enough to apologize if you have not come to a clear understanding of your offense. It is not even enough to be sincerely sorry for your wrong if you have no plans to change your behavior.

Repentance requires humility, an attitude few of us enjoy embracing. You have to be willing to see yourself in truth, a reality that will humble both the heathen and the upright. Since none of us are without sin, none of us have the right to look down our noses at the faults of others. Even if we were without sin, we would still need to follow Jesus' example by laying down our rights so that we can be reconciled in our relationships.

Humility in repentance involves confessing your sin to the one you offended, agreeing that what you did was wrong, and then actively choosing to behave or respond in ways that will keep you from offending again. Of course there will be occasions when you slip back into an old sin pattern. Ask for grace when this happens. If, however, you continue through life with no intention to rise above that offense, you have not truly repented.

Beyond repentance, we have learned an even deeper level of humility that has averted offense time and again. Because we have a covenant perspective of marriage – laying down our rights and picking up all the responsibilities – our interaction with one another is much more courteous. We don't approach conversation with the intent to attack, and our discussions don't consist of defensive statements meant to protect ourselves. If I see that Robert has been offended by what I've said, I willingly apologize even if I don't see that I've said anything wrong. If Debbie responds to me out of frustration with the kids, I don't huff and blame her for taking it out on me, the innocent victim. Instead, I lovingly remind her that I am on her side. Soft answers turn away wrath instead of stirring up anger (Proverbs 15:1). It is more important to me that his needs are met; it is more important to me that her feelings aren't hurt.

Forgiveness, humility and repentance stoke the fires of marriage. In order for your relationship to burn for a lifetime, it has to be tended constantly. Unforgiveness, pride and stubbornness are like buckets of water tossed on the flames.

Refuse to let such sins extinguish the blaze of your marriage. Satan will stop at nothing to see the last embers of your life together burn out. Thankfully, "He who is in you is greater than he who is in the world" (1 John 4:4). By following Christ's teaching and example, by committing to a relationship that images God, you are guaranteeing success and blessing for your union.

Through prayer, Terri received the mind of Christ regarding her failing marriage. She saw how damaging her spirit of unforgiveness had been to their relationship. Finally, she realized that not only was she bound by unforgiveness, but that she was holding Frank in bondage as well. In her own words, Terri confessed: "The Lord dealt mightily with my heart. I realized forgiveness was a decision. It didn't have anything to do with how I felt wronged. That task of forgiving, which once seemed impossible, suddenly became easier."

Terri went to Frank and repented of her unwillingness to forgive. At that point, miracles began happening in their family. Their middle son, the one struggling with asthma, was healed. Their other son, the one needing intense surgery, received a report from his doctor indicating no need for surgery at all. And, maybe the most amazing healing of all, Frank and Terri never got divorced. Peace came over their home, and their marriage was completely reconciled. New life had been released through Terri and Frank's choice to forgive one another. Frank and Terri are leaders in our church. They have allowed us to use their real names because they love to tell their story and give God all of the glory He deserves.

If you are holding onto a multitude of wounds from your spouse, let them go. Healing will never come if you continue to sip the poison. Choose to walk in forgiveness so that life-giving power will be released in your marriage. As you forgive, so will you be forgiven, by God and likely by your spouse as well. It is much easier to forgive someone who has forgiven you in the past. Neither of you is perfect, and each of you needs consistent grace from the other.

When you wrong the one you love, humbly repent of your actions. Confess to the selfishness that broke your marriage's covenant and then lay down your rights and pick up the responsibility to love. Prayerfully receive the forgiveness given by God and by your spouse. Finally, walk in that forgiveness, refusing to give into shame or guilt.

Remember Ruth Bell Graham's advice: Successful marriage is the union of two good forgivers. Conflict doesn't have to drive a wedge between you. Instead, let it drive you to deeper levels of grace and humility. And just like your relationship with Christ abounds in goodness because of the forgiveness He bestowed on you, so will goodness flow through your mutually forgiving relationship . . . your blessed marriage.

CHAPTER 10

Heaven on Earth

The couple glides across the floor with ease and grace. Harmoniously the pair dances, twirling, dipping and sashaying in perfect rhythm. Like an image from a refined painting, they complement one another beautifully. The gentleman holds her firmly, yet tenderly, as he guides her through elegant and sometimes daring steps. She looks into his eyes adoringly, trusting his direction and yielding to his lead. His strength supports her delicate frame, and her splendor boasts of his tasteful agility. Though he doesn't speak, she knows his direction, and though she doesn't ask, he knows her intention.

Spectators encircle, creating a stage on which the mesmerizing duo captivates the onlookers with their romance, skill and flawless performance. No one in the crowd notices the intricacies of this partnership: his leadership and her yielding. All they see is beauty, the connection of two individuals moving as one with poise and style.

The blessed marriage is a dance much like this one, flowing smoothly because it is what God intended it to be. As the man lovingly leads his wife through life, she honors his direction by following. The two experience intimacy so deep that words are not even needed to communicate their hearts. To the world, they display the harmonious posture of their Creator and Lord.

Amazingly, when a crowd gathers to watch a well-performed dance, there is never a comment about the man's domineering methods or the lady's doormat submission. No, everyone remains awestruck at the couple's envious connection to one another. When the roles are respected and obeyed, the two become like one, moving with purpose, skill and accomplishment.

Blessing waits for your marriage, even if you are just learning to dance with one another. Yes, first you have to die to self, to your agenda and rights. Yes, you have to place utmost priority on your spouse. Yes, you have to assume all of the duties to love, honor and submit. Men, you have to learn to communicate and take responsibility. Women, you have to satisfy his sexual needs and lavish honor upon him. And, when your spouse isn't doing his part, you have to forgive, trust God and pray for him. It may seem like a lot of work, but once you begin this dance, you will discover heaven on earth.

God always honors obedience. When you live out your marriage in covenant, He is pleased. And like a proud daddy who buys his son ice cream after he mows the lawn for the first time, our Father lavishly pours out blessings on those of us who honor His instructions for marriage.

Bearing Fruit

God's first command to Adam and Eve was to be fruitful and multiply (Genesis 1:28). His original plan was not to have one man and one woman made in His image to rule over the whole earth. No, His plan was to have a whole race of people who looked like Him. Instead of populating the earth Himself, He included Adam and Eve in that process. He told them to bear offspring that look like Him.

It is impossible to reproduce by yourself. Even the birds and the bees know that it takes two. Two must come together and become one before there can be offspring. Man and woman were commissioned by God Himself to come together and to produce children that look like God. What an amazing task and great reward for coming together!

Even beyond coming together to have children though, God wants our fruit-bearing to extend to other areas of life. Mankind is the only one that bears the image of God, but other works communicate His truth, love and goodness to the world as well. An amazing principle has been proven over and over in marriages, families, teams and organizations: While one can overcome a thousand, two can overcome ten thousand (Deuteronomy 32). Coming together in unity toward one common goal causes exponential growth in the output!

I (Robert) have had an amazingly fruitful ministry over the past twenty-five years. Experience and God's Word have taught me why it has been so fruitful . . . I've been right with God, and I've been right with Debbie. Even though Debbie is not a preacher like I am, the partnership we have in life and the unity of direction that we maintain in ministry have brought exponential growth to those things we have attempted for God, including my preaching. The Lord looks at the integrity of our marriage and blesses me with an anointing that bears overflowing fruit.

Consider the ministry of the apostle Paul. Though Paul was not married, he did travel and minister with a team. In the entire book of Acts, detailing the four missionary journeys of Paul and his associates, there is only one city Paul went to alone. Attempting to escape angry mobs in Berea, Paul went ahead of his group to Athens to wait for them to join him. Of course, as outspoken and bold as he was, he could not wait there idly. Paul began sharing the gospel openly with both Jews and Gentiles. One message he delivered there is considered to be one of his finest, often quoted and referred to today. But, despite his eloquence and enthusiasm, no church was planted in Athens (Acts 17:15-34). Every other city Paul preached in and ministered to with his team received the birth of a new church. Athens, however, did not.

In his ministry, Paul learned the necessity of partnership to see fruit. In fact, there is one occurrence when Paul felt led by the Spirit to go to a certain place, but he did not go because he did not have Titus with him (2 Corinthians 2:12-13). He knew that his best chances for reaching people came when he ministered with a team.

Husband and wife, your blessed marriage can produce

fruit in your life that you never imagined possible. When you dream together, work together, pray together and serve together, exponential blessing will be poured out on you, and life will spring up abundantly. We will go so far as to say that when the two of you are led by the Spirit of God to accomplish something together, nothing will be held back from you.

Remember the story of the Tower of Babel in Genesis 11? All of mankind had come together with one language and one purpose: to build a great city and tower to heaven in order to create a name for themselves lest they be scattered over the face of the earth. God's response to their plans was to confuse their language so that they would be forced to disperse. He knew that with the power they had in unity, nothing they proposed to do would be withheld from them (Genesis 11:1-9). At this point in history, Christ had not yet died to redeem the purposes of man's heart, thus, their plans would only lead to corruption and destruction. He had to thwart their efforts so that His plan for truth and life could be realized.

Several thousand years later, another group of people came together under one language and purpose, and God did not thwart their plans. In Acts 2 we see Jesus' disciples gathered together when the Holy Spirit fell upon them, giving them the gift of speaking in tongues. Jesus already had commissioned them to take the gospel to the world, and once they had the promised empowering of the Holy Spirit, they set out to accomplish Jesus' purpose. As the book of Acts continues, it records the tremendous success of the early church. Miracles were plentiful, as they saw people raised from the dead, many healed and multitudes saved. Today, church growth experts look at the early church and try to pinpoint the source of its amazing success. Most of the time they miss it . . . The early church was so fruitful because it was unified!

What about you? Do people look at your life and wonder at the tremendous fruitfulness? Are you and your spouse bound together under one purpose? With the help of your husband or wife, you could accomplish ten times more than what you struggle to accomplish alone. Come together as one. Pray. Dream. Take each other's hand, and step onto the path of abundant blessing and fruit.

Fulfill Your Potential

Today's technology is amazing. Have you seen those all-in-one machines that can print, copy, fax and scan? If you went out and bought such a contraption, took it home, hooked it up and then used it every day to fax letters to your boss, would you be getting your money's worth? Absolutely not. If the machine can also print, copy and scan, you should use it to its fullest capacity.

God created you to accomplish many purposes as well.

In all likelihood, you've discovered quite a few already in life. You are a businessman. You are a teacher. You are a deacon at church. You are a volunteer at the local community center. God has packed you so full of potential that it will take your whole lifetime to discover it all. One particular role that you may not realize you were equipped to play in life, however, is the one where you help your spouse reach his or her full potential.

In chapter two, we explained that man was designed to reach his full potential with the help of woman, and woman was designed to reach her full potential with the help of man. Your spouse's ability to do all he or she was created to do rests on how much you help. Now, since this is what God equipped you to do, it is part of your destiny as well. You will never reach your full potential unless you live up to your responsibility in your spouse's life. This is ultimately like a big circle. You help him reach his potential and in doing so you reach yours. He helps you reach your potential and likewise, he reaches his.

Are we ever more satisfied in life than when we are living up to our fullest potential? Marriage gives you the opportunity to be fulfilled in life. There is joy in watching your wife become all she was gifted to become, but there is contentment in becoming all you were created to be as well.

Men, remember, you are her source for all that she needs in life. That is your function. That is your calling. Women, remember, you are a life-giver to his dreams and goals. That is your gifting. That is your calling. Help your spouse live up to his or her potential so that you too can become all that God intended you to be.

Reap the Rewards

Perhaps the most natural benefits of the blessed marriage come when your spouse responds to your godly actions and attitudes with equally godly actions and attitudes. As we have mentioned before, a loving husband can heal a dishonoring wife, and an honoring wife can heal an unloving husband. When you die to yourself and move toward the other in love, honor and submission, he or she will take notice. And while you might not see an immediate change, over time the reactions to your godliness will take the form of godliness as well.

When you first got married, it was like you moved onto a farm at harvest season . . . you ate a crop you didn't plant. After a lifetime of teaching, experiences, pain and memories, you jumped into his or her life and tasted the sweetness and bitterness that had been baked in. Everyone comes into marriage with some kind of baggage . . . for me (Debbie), it was insecurity; for me (Robert), it was insensitivity. That baggage makes coexistence difficult and harmony almost impossible at times! But you only have to eat that crop for a season. As soon as you marry, you begin planting seeds into the other's life. When those seeds sprout, you will be forced to deal with the crop you produce. Following the path of the blessed marriage, you plant seeds of love and kindness that will develop into a crop of intimacy and tenderness. What sweeter reward in marriage is there than tender intimacy?

Allow us to give you a few practical examples of planting positive seeds into your spouse's life. Gentlemen, remember when we talked about a woman's need for affection? The more affectionate you are, the more sexual she will become. Ladies, remember when we talked about honoring your husband as the king of his castle? The more you treat him like a king, the more he will treat you like a queen. Husbands, when you meet her need for security, she will blossom into a respectful and adoring wife. Wives, when you meet his need for companionship, he will surprise you with invitations that prove his love for you. Guys, when you open up to her probing questions, she will be drawn to your sincerity and cling closer to your side than ever before. Girls, when you submit to his leadership, he has the opportunity to show off his strength and lead you in godliness.

Every action invites a reaction. When your loving actions meet your spouse's loving reactions, you will discover a life that is heaven on earth. God's divine intent for marriage was that two people, dead to self, would live to meet the needs of the other so that all needs are met, not selfishly, but selflessly.

Husbands should look like Christ. Wives also should look like Christ. When two people who look like Christ live together, their union is heaven on earth.

An Example for the World to See

After twenty-six years of marriage, we can look back and remember the godly couples that represented the blessed marriage to us. Their wise counsel instructed us in righteous paths but more poignant was their daily example. Even today, we watch these beautiful relationships and glean godly principles from their lives that we too can implement in order to invite even more of God's blessing in.

If you have never watched the brilliance of a blessed marriage up close, it is probably hard for you to imagine that this kind of marriage is even possible. We encourage you to find such an example to follow in your own marriage. Ask God to show you a couple who can mentor and train you in the art of holy relationship. If you already have a blessed marriage, look around your community and find a young couple who could benefit from your experience and coaching.

For those of you who already have children, please know that they are looking to you to teach them what their future marriage should look like. They may not realize it, but their whole perspective on relationships will be formed by what you model for them. Even more urgent though in their lives is the need for godly parents whose deep love for one another provides a stable home and future for them. When the storms of life inevitably come their way, they need to have the anchor of a healthy family to get them through.

Having a blessed marriage transcends your own personal happiness or fulfillment. God designed marriage to image Him, to present His unique characteristics to the world in picture form so that people could understand and embrace Him. You are that picture to your family, your community, your church, and whoever else is watching that you aren't even aware of. What an awesome privilege to display our Father to a world in desperate need of His love!

If the Future Looks Bleak . . .

A couple once approached Robert for marriage counseling. When Robert and I met with them, we listened to their story that went something like this: "We have grown up in church and were saved as children. We come from good homes, and our pastor was the founder of one of the best marriage ministries in the country. We have been to numerous marriage seminars both before and after we were married."

She told us, "I know that I should honor my husband, and I also know that I'm not doing it."

He told us, "I know that I should put her needs first in our relationship, but I'm not doing that either."

They shared one marriage principle after another that they had learned but were not doing. After about an hour of listening, Robert leaned forward and said, "I'm going to tell you something that I've never told any other couple in over twenty years of marriage counseling."

I remember thinking to myself, "Boy, I can't wait to hear this. What words of wisdom is he about to impart that can fix this messed up marriage? I'm really going to listen well so that I can pass this advice on to others who are struggling in marriage."

Then, he uttered words that I will never forget: "I can't help you." With that, he leaned back in his chair and just looked at the couple. We were all stunned and silent.

Before I had a chance to question Robert's comment, the husband spoke up and asked, "What do you mean, you can't help us?"

Robert answered, "When people have problems, they go to their pastors for help. He gives them some answers that they didn't already know, and then they apply that knowledge to their situations and it works. You, on the other hand, already know all the right answers, but you are not doing it. You don't have a knowledge problem . . . you have a rebellion problem. The only thing wrong with your marriage is that you (looking at the husband) won't love her the way Christ loves the church, and you (looking at the wife) won't honor him as you would honor the Lord. But you already know this, so I can't help you!" With that, he led us all in prayer and ended the meeting.

The young couple thanked us for our time and left. In their car, before even leaving the parking lot, the husband turned to his wife with tears in his eyes and said, "He's right, and I am so sorry!" They talked for about 45 minutes, crying and praying together, and in those moments, their marriage took a turn for the better.

Now, more that five years later, she is on our staff, and he is one of our deacons. To watch their marriage today, you would never know that it was once in dire conditions. They have an amazingly blessed marriage because they both took responsibility to obey the instruction they had received from God's Word.

This may be difficult to admit, but you may not have a marriage problem . . . you may have a rebellion problem. If you know the right things to do but are not doing them, the answer for you is simple. Start doing what you already know to do and then leave the rest up to God! We don't want to sound harsh, but we do want to push you into obedience that will usher blessing into your marriage.

If the blessed marriage still seems far beyond your reach because you have a spouse who is not willing to obey and do his or her part, remember, you can be the redeemer in the relationship. Jesus did this for you. He redeemed us even when we were in rebellion. He died first! When you die first, you can trust God to bring the blessing. If you fear entering a covenant where you pick up all the responsibilities because you wonder how your own needs will be met, again, trust God to meet those needs. He can take care of you far better than you can take care of yourself. He knows what you need more than you do.

Years ago, Robert returned home after a long ministry trip. He was only scheduled to be home for a few days before he had to leave again. The children and I were so excited to see him and spend time with him. Only a few minutes after getting home, a friend of his called and invited him to play golf. While I knew he really needed some recreation time, I also knew his family needed to be with him too. When he asked me if he could go, I tried to hide my disappointment and told him to go ahead. I figured that the whole family could spend the evening together. In my heart, I tried to be happy for him and not say anything that would spoil his day.

Within minutes, he was gone. As soon as he walked out the door, though, he got a headache. From what he tells me, he knew God wasn't pleased with his decision to go, but he was still determined to meet his friend. His headache grew more intense, and before he got to the course, he had to stop and buy some pain killers. By the time he actually started playing, Robert felt horrible. He lasted only to the fourth tee when his vision grew blurry and he vomited all over the green. (If you're not a golfer, it's a bad thing to vomit on a green!)

Defeated, Robert gave up. On his way home, God began to deal with him. Specifically, the Lord told him to come home and repent to me. Apparently, Robert fought that instruction, telling God he was sorry but that it would really hurt his pride if he had to ask for forgiveness. Well, God didn't let him off that easily. He proceeded to tell Robert not only to apologize but also to ask me to pray for his healing. At that point I think Robert considered keeping the headache.

He surprised me with his early arrival home and shocked me even more with the story of his headache. By God's grace, I didn't say anything that I regretted but instead offered him some medicine. Refusing the medicine, he asked me to sit next to him on the sofa. After sharing his conversation with God, he confessed his selfishness and asked for forgiveness. Willingly, I forgave him. Then, he asked me to pray for his healing. As I did, God immediately healed Robert's headache. We spent the rest of the day as a family, enjoying one another's company.

Had I complained or sulked when Robert asked to go play golf, he probably would have stayed home. But he would have relented begrudgingly. By responding to him in love and trusting God to change his heart, the situation turned out far better. Today I look back and see this event as a turning point in Robert's growth as a husband. He knows that I trust God with him, and He also knows that God is looking out for me. Robert treats me with love and priority because God taught him to do so.

We have come a long way. God has been so good to us through every step: disciplining, teaching, forgiving and rewarding. The opportunity to write this book is another overwhelming blessing to us. To think that God took us from an unstable stage of immaturity, insecurity and insensitivity, to a place where we can teach others how to have a godly marriage is . . . amazing. We have nothing to boast about though, because we know, more than anyone else, that it is only responding to the grace of God that has gotten us this far. Our marriage is blessed because we both learned to die. When we died we went to heaven . . . heaven on earth.

Our Father does not show favoritism among His children. The blessings we have come to know are available to you as well. Intimacy, fruitfulness and fulfillment can all be yours when you choose to die. *Any* and *every* marriage can be a blessed marriage if both partners would choose to die to selfishness and instead live to please and serve the other.

In God's Kingdom, death always brings life . . . and the life it brings is always better than the life that was laid down. Go ahead and die. Heaven is waiting for you.

Endnotes

CHAPTER 3
1. John Maxwell, *The 21 Irrefutable Laws of Leadership* (Nashville, TN: Thomas Nelson, 1998).

CHAPTER 6
1. *Biblesoft's Nelson's Illustrated Bible Dictionary.* CD-ROM. Biblesoft and Thomas Nelson Publishers, 2004.
2. *Biblesoft's The International Standard Bible Encyclopedia.* CD-ROM. Biblesoft and Hendrickson Publishers, 2004.
3. *Biblesoft's McClintock and Strong Encyclopedia.* CD-ROM. Biblesoft, 2000.
4. Jimmy Evans, *Marriage on the Rock* (Dallas, TX: Marriage Today, 1994).

CHAPTER 7
1. Jimmy Evans, *Marriage on the Rock* (Dallas, TX: Marriage Today, 1994).
2. Gary and Barbara Rosberg. *The Five Love Needs of Men and Women* (Colorado Springs, CO: Alive Communications, 2000).
3. Jack W. Hayford, *Sex and the Single Soul.* (Ventura, CA: Regal Books, 2005).
4. Linda Dillow and Lorraine Pintus. *Intimate Issues.* (Colorado Springs, CO: WaterBrook Press, 1999).
5. WB&A Market Research survey, "Survey for the National Sleep Foundation," March 2005. www.sleepfoundation.org

CHAPTER 8
1. *Biblesoft's Hitchcock's Bible Names Dictionary.* CD-ROM. Biblesoft, 2004.
2. *Biblesoft's The New Unger's Bible Dictionary.* CD-ROM. Biblesoft and Moody Press, 2004.

CPSIA information can be obtained
at www.ICGtesting.com
Printed in the USA
FFOW03n0816070418
46147360-47288FF